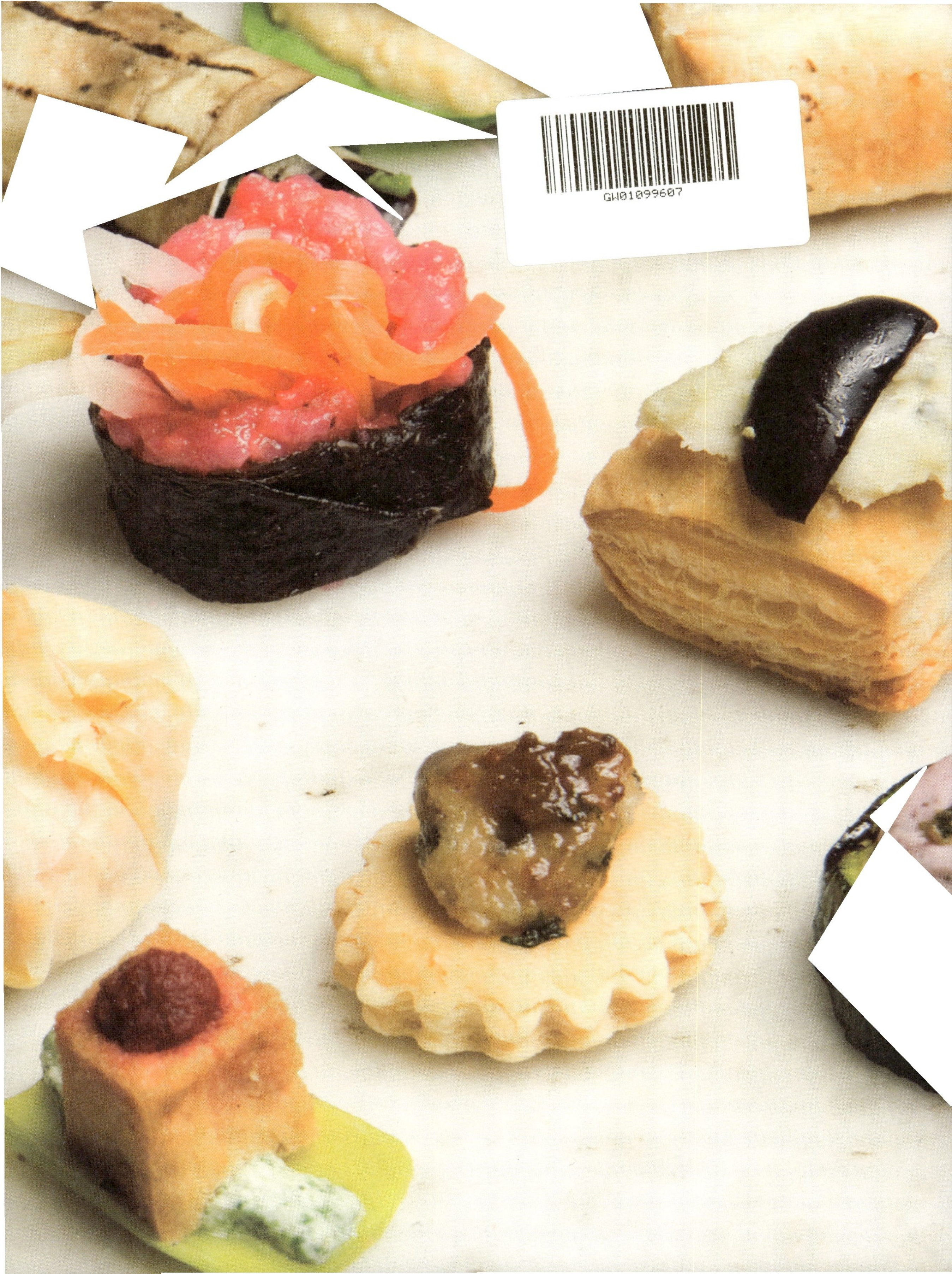

food for friends

This book is dedicated to our parents

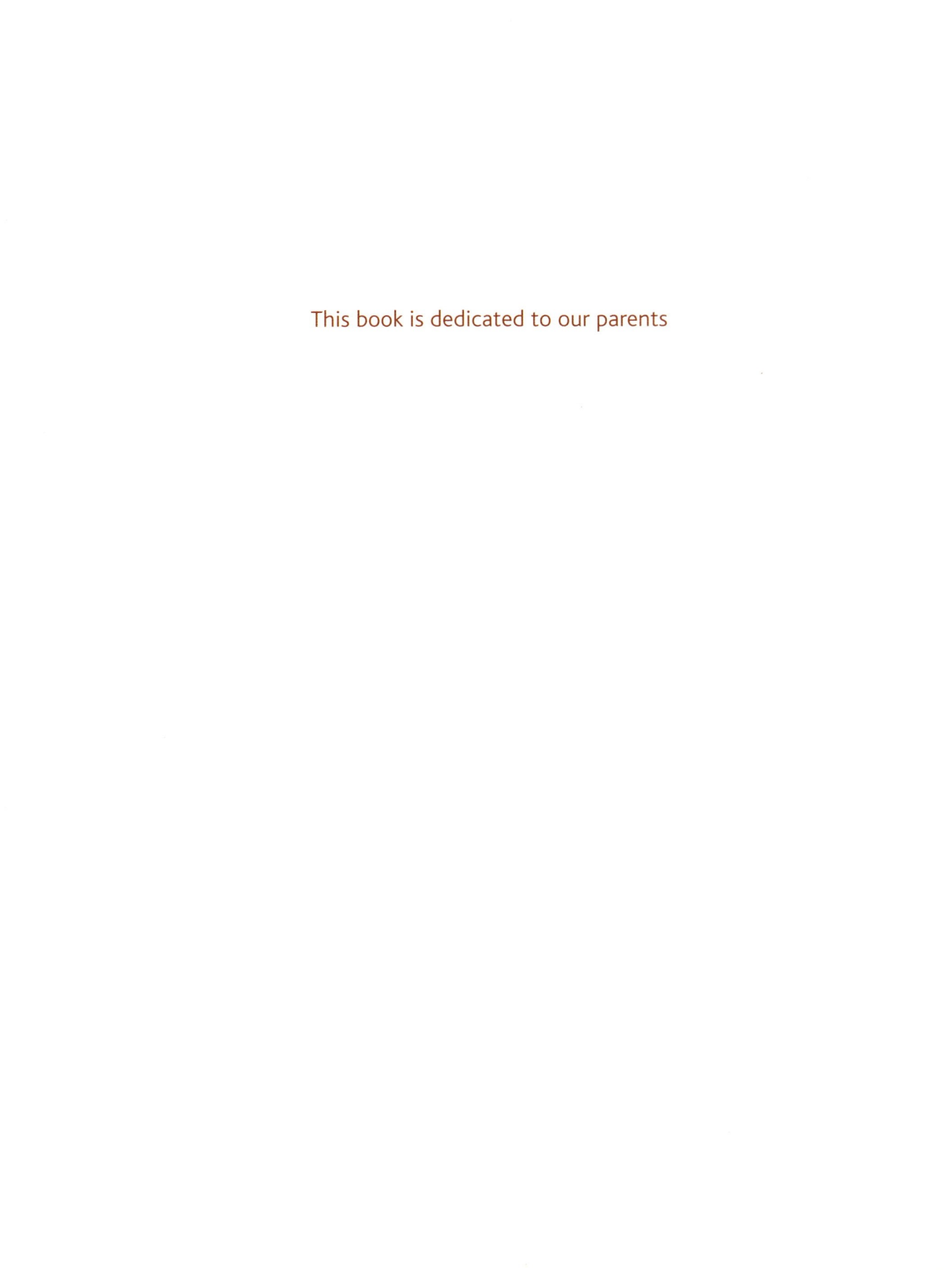

food for friends

MODERN VEGETARIAN COOKING AT HOME

Jane and Ramin Mostowfi
with Kalil Resende

Photographs by Adrian Peacock

Serving sizes vary, but all spoon measures in the recipes are level and eggs are medium in size unless otherwise described; oven temperatures are for conventional ovens. If you wish to make a dish for a different number of people, you may need to adjust the cooking times as well as the quantties. Cooking times are broad guidelines – hobs and ovens vary; pan and dish sizes can have an impact too. When it comes down to it, trust your judgement and your knowledge of your own kitchen.

All eggs used are free-range or organic and all wine and cheeses in the recipes are vegetarian.

Copyright © Jane and Ramin Mostowfi, 2010
The right of Jane and Ramin Mostowfi to be identified as the authors of this book has been asserted in accordance with the Copyright, Designs and Patents Act 1988.

First published in 2010 by
Infinite Ideas Limited
36 St Giles
Oxford
OX1 3LD
United Kingdom
www.infideas.com

Reprinted 2011

All rights reserved. Except for the quotation of small passages for the purposes of criticism or review, no part of this publication may be reproduced, stored in a retrieval system or transmitted in any form or by any means, electronic, mechanical, photocopying, recording, scanning or otherwise, except under the terms of the Copyright, Designs and Patents Act 1988 or under the terms of a licence issued by the Copyright Licensing Agency Ltd, 90 Tottenham Court Road, London W1T 4LP, UK, without the permission in writing of the publisher. Requests to the publisher should be addressed to the Permissions Department, Infinite Ideas Limited, 36 St Giles, Oxford, OX1 3LD, UK, or faxed to +44 (0) 1865 514777.

A CIP catalogue record for this book is available from the British Library

ISBN 978-1-906821-54-8

Brand and product names are trademarks or registered trademarks of their respective owners.

Cover designed by D.R.ink
Text designed and typeset by Nicki Averill
Photographs by Adrian Peacock
Printed and bound in India

Contents

Acknowledgements vii
Introduction ix

Basics 1
Salads 17
Soups 29
Light bites 39
Pastas and bakes 51
Noodles, grains and pulses 67
Fritters, galettes and burgers 77
Parcels, tarts, soufflés and stuffed veggies 101
Big pots and slow cooking 115
Special occasions 129
Desserts 137
Baking 159

Index 171

← THE LANES ⇐

Acknowledgements

We would like to thank the many people who have helped make this book possible. They tested recipes, let us into their kitchens to take photographs, lent us dishes and forgave us when they got broken! Thank you Lucy, Amanda, Caroline, Marjan, Noushin, John and Karen.

A big thank you to Mum and Friday; without your help buying the business, none of this would have happened. Thank you to all our staff for your support and dedication. Thank you Dad, for your constant encouragement whilst writing this book. Thanks go to our photographer, Adrian Peacock, for his patience and help. Finally we would like to thank Kalil for his taste buds, imagination and his help in bringing all these recipes together.

food for friends

established 1981

www.foodforfriends.com
tel: 01273 202310

Introduction

Two weeks before Christmas in December 2004, armed with a lot of enthusiasm, energy, a huge bank loan and, looking back now, a certain amount of naivety, Ramin and I took over Food for Friends restaurant in Brighton. We had spent a couple of years looking for a business to take over, something that we could turn around and make our own. We both had professional careers in the corporate world and at the time I was on maternity leave with our daughter Lily and our two year old son Sam – but we knew that if we didn't take the step at that point, we never would. And so we did. We gave up our jobs, found help to look after the children and plunged straight in, working tirelessly back to back, seven days a week, to put our own stamp on Food for Friends.

We have had some fantastic members of staff along the way who have helped shape both the restaurant and its food. We have certainly encountered some very steep learning curves over the years but, with a great bunch of staff and the support of many amazing customers, we truly believe this is what has made Food for Friends the much-loved Brighton restaurant that it is today.

The restaurant was founded in 1981 with the ethos of serving global vegetarian cuisine that was not 'just a load of old lentils'. It was a place that Brighton's mix of eclectic locals knew and loved. It was a regular occurrence to see scores of hungry people queuing around the building, all waiting to order their lunch at the infamous Food for Friends counter.

Food for Friends is still enjoying the same level of popularity but for different reasons. When Ramin and I took over the restaurant in 2004 we wanted to bring this popular Brighton restaurant up to date. Our customers told us that they wanted to have a relaxed, friendly and comfortable environment to eat good food in, as they felt that they had outgrown the hippy café which was the Food for Friends of the 80s and 90s.

Kalil joined us in the summer of 2005, six months after we bought the restaurant. Over the years his talent, confidence and love of vegetarian food grew tremendously. He always experimented with new ideas and tried out ways to make dishes adaptable for dietary intolerances without involving substitute foods.

Now, in the restaurant's thirtieth year, we have firmly established ourselves as a Brighton institution. Many of our customers are second generation; parents bring their children here while reminiscing about their student days at Food for Friends, and some are now even bringing their grandchildren. We may have given the restaurant a couple of facelifts and refreshed the brand, but the basic concept remains the same: innovative and delicious dishes that keep not only vegetarians but all lovers of good food coming back, year after year. Our extensive customer base tells us that many have been coming to us on a regular basis for more than thirty years.

Our ethos remains simple. We believe in supporting local producers whenever possible, using the finest and freshest seasonal ingredients to deliver high quality, great value food. For those with specific dietary requirements we offer gluten-free and/or vegan options for most of our dishes. The restaurant is warm and welcoming, offering a relaxed and unpretentious gourmet dining experience where customers pay for good food, not freshly pressed linen.

When we decided to write this cookery book, while knowing that it would be a great tool for people cooking for a special dietary requirement at home, we also wanted to bear in mind those who simply enjoy good vegetarian cooking. We want to be able to share the fact that the flavours of herbs and spices come through much more clearly in meatless dishes, and the personalities of vegetables and grains are much more vivid. With so many tantalising food combinations and spice mixes from all over the world, meatless eating can be a culinary adventure.

During the last ten years, and especially in vegetarian cooking, there has been a move away from heavy, stodgy foods. An interest and trend to infuse and entwine Middle-Eastern, Mediterranean and Asian flavours and ingredients has made veggie food far more appealing to a much wider audience – and many of these influences are naturally and deliciously vegetarian. The Middle East, China, Vietnam and India are just a few of the places where vegetables, grains and spices play a larger culinary role than meat does. As a child, the only rice that seemed to be available was American long-grain rice, which used to be boiled up and really tasted of nothing. But look on the shelves now: jasmine to basmati, arborio to paella. And there's lemon grass, bulgar, pomegranate, rice noodles, bok choy, shiitake mushrooms and flavoured oils… With the influx of people from varying cultures comes a need for readily available ingredients that are used in all these styles of cooking, meaning that we are able to easily infuse all of these new flavours into our daily cooking.

Our food also seems to appeal to a rapidly growing new market sector called the 'meat reducers', people who eat more of a vegetarian diet because of the perception that eating less meat is much healthier. These types of customers tell us that they enjoy our food because they can have three courses without feeling guilty.

On a more serious note, there are an increasing number of people with food intolerances spanning from serious life-threatening conditions to the milder food allergies and sensitivities that cause discomfort. Alarmingly, the food industry does not seem to be reacting to these intolerances to reflect this change. In our restaurant, customers often thank us for providing a menu that makes them feel 'normal' and not a 'fussy eater', for being a place where they can bring their friends and family safe in the knowledge that everyone will enjoy good food without feeling they are compromising.

Whether you are dairy intolerant or have religious restrictions to your diet, or whether your diet is wheat- or gluten-free, or vegan, we believe that with this cookbook there need no longer be any obstacles to great food. We know that when we found out our daughter had a mild intolerance to gluten it was quite daunting; we not only had to think about what we were cooking for her in a family environment, but about how she was being fed at school, at parties and in other people's houses. And this is the same for adults with intolerances. Food is central to so many social situations, and problems can make people feel alienated and cause anxiety for the individuals affected and for their hosts.

Dealing with dietary needs is much more straightforward than a lot of people think. One of the features of our book is that many recipes are dairy and/or gluten-free, and that simple adjustments are often suggested for adapting dishes to specific diets. It shows the reader that adapting these dishes is not that difficult when you have the know-how.

This book is a collection of our customers' favourite recipes. Luckily for them, lots of our dishes are focused around the fusion of really good flavours, and not fussy cooking techniques. Our approach is understated; something we believe comes from a confident kitchen team. In fact, any new dish that evolves in the Food for Friends kitchen goes on a journey through staff trials and the daily specials board. Then, after lots of prodding customers for feedback, it may make its way onto the à la carte menu. The recipes we have chosen for the cookbook are not just the ones we think have been our most successful dishes, but those that have proved to be the biggest hits with our customers (the ones that have the most recipe requests).

A vital part of good vegetarian cooking lies in seasoning and flavours. It takes a little more thought to make food without meat flavoursome, but with some basic techniques it is very simple. Today it is much easier to eat a vegetarian diet as the variety of foods available is greater now than ever before. Products that ten years ago were nearly impossible to find in the UK are now readily available in our supermarkets.

Our book brings together many exotic elements along with British comfort foods we all know and love, because – as at the restaurant – we would like to share with you our repertoire of the more ethnic dishes and the use of ingredients which we have collected in our travels to many different countries around the world. These also come from my mother whose passion for cooking was influenced by her Malaysian husband, and from Ramin's mum and his Aunt Susan who formed a love of good Persian food in both me and Ramin. And there's my dad, who has taken us to many wonderful restaurants over the years so we really developed a palate and an understanding of what good food is about.

We hope that, through our recipes and the supporting material, this book will give our readers the confidence to go and experiment with vegetarian cooking themselves.

Ramin and Jane xx
Enjoy!

> V – vegan;
> VO – vegan option;
> GF – gluten-free;
> GFO – gluten-free option;
> N – contains nuts;
> S – contains sesame seeds.

Flavoured oils, page 10

Basics

V, GF
Vegetable Stock

Home-made stock creates a much better flavour, especially when cooking vegetarian food. Too many stocks are insipid or taste too much of one ingredient. The stock recipe we use will provide good body and depth of flavour for a dish but should not dominate it. Strong root vegetables such as turnips and parsnips are not good additions, and neither are potatoes or cabbage as they can be too overpowering and give the stock a soup-like texture. Although you should always use the freshest ingredients for your stock you can still add bits and pieces which are lurking in your vegetable cupboard, but remember to wash everything first or you will end up with a gritty stock.

The characteristics of a good stock are fine flavour and clarity. Guard against over-seasoning, as boiling concentrates the saltiness. When your stock is simmering give it an occasional stir and skim off the scum which will form on the top. Make sure that you don't cover your stockpot completely as the stock needs to reduce by boiling and evaporation. Finally, when you go to all the trouble of making your own stock it's a good idea to make up more than you need and then freeze it in manageable quantities.

Makes 2–3 litres

1 large onion, quartered
2 large carrots, quartered
1 small bunch of celery, coarsely chopped (including leaves)
2 leeks, white parts only, halved lengthways, rinsed and halved again
1 butternut squash, deseeded, skin on
2 tomatoes, halved and deseeded
1 cos lettuce, coarsely chopped
3 cloves of garlic, peeled
1 dried red chilli
4 fresh bay leaves
a handful of parsley stalks, crushed
half a lemon, sliced
6 black peppercorns
salt to taste

Put all the ingredients in a large stockpot. Add water to cover (approximately 4 litres), and bring to the boil. As soon as it boils, reduce the heat and allow to simmer for 15 minutes. Stir the stock and skim off the scum, then continue to cook at a simmer for at least an hour, skimming the top regularly.

Remove the pan from the heat and strain the stock through a fine sieve into a large bowl. Once everything has cooled, discard the contents of the sieve. When the stock has cooled completely, refrigerate it for several hours before using. The stock will keep in the fridge for up to three days or for up to three months in the freezer, in small batches.

V
Red Pepper Sauce

This is a very simple and versatile dairy-free sauce. In the restaurant we use it for our gratins and pasta dishes, and as a savoury coulis to decorate plates.

Makes 300ml

2 red peppers
2 yellow peppers
1 tbsp tomato purée
4 cloves of garlic, mashed
2 tsp balsamic vinegar
2 tsp red wine vinegar
8 tbsp extra virgin olive oil
salt and pepper

Preheat the oven to 180°C/gas mark 4. Put the peppers on a baking tray and roast them in the oven until the pepper has started to blacken on the outside. Take them out of the oven and place them in a sealed plastic bag until they have cooled down, then take them out of the bag and peel them. Cut off the stem, remove the seeds and the white bits inside. Put the peppers, tomato purée, garlic, vinegars, oil and seasoning in a blender and purée everything together. Cover the mixture until needed.

V
Basic tomato sauce

A quick-cooking tomato sauce is indispensable; not only can it be used on pizza and pasta but also with vegetables and risottos. In the warmer months use fresh, juicy tomatoes; in the winter, choose canned Italian plum tomatoes. Just remember that the tastier the tomato, the tastier your sauce. You can make double the quantity and freeze a batch for another day.

Serves 4

450g ripe tomatoes, or 2 x 400g tins of plum tomatoes
1 onion, peeled
1 medium carrot, peeled
125g celery
1 tbsp olive oil
1 large clove of garlic, crushed
1 tbsp mixed fresh herbs (such as parsley, basil, thyme, marjoram), finely chopped
1 dried bay leaf
15ml tomato purée
150ml dry white wine or vegetable stock
salt and pepper
3 sprigs of basil, stalks removed

To skin fresh tomatoes make a cross on the bottom of each one, plunge it into boiling water for five seconds and then immediately into a bowl of iced water. Peel off the skin. Chop them finely and discard the seeds. Finely chop the onion, carrot and celery. Heat the oil in the saucepan and sauté the onion, carrot, celery, garlic and herbs until soft. Stir in the tomatoes, bay leaf, tomato purée, wine or stock and seasoning. Bring to the boil, cover and simmer for 15–20 minutes or until the vegetables are tender. Then uncover the pan and allow the sauce to reduce and thicken a little; discard the bay leaf. Tear up the basil leaves and add them.

If you want a smoother texture, purée the sauce in a blender or food processor.

Options
V, GF

Roasted tomato sauce

Place 450g whole fresh tomatoes in a roasting tin or baking tray in a cosy single layer. Drizzle them generously with olive oil (we use our garlic-infused oil). Season with salt and pepper and add a couple of splashes of red wine vinegar. Put the tray in a hot oven (200°C/gas mark 6) for approximately 30 minutes until the skins begin to colour and peel away. Take the tray out and remove the tomato skins, then use the roasted tomatoes instead of the fresh or tinned ones in the recipe above.

V, GF

Chilli tomato sauce

Prepare the tomatoes as for the roasted tomato sauce, but add some chilli-infused oil or scatter a chopped whole fresh chilli (or a teaspoon of crushed dried chillies) over the tomatoes before roasting.

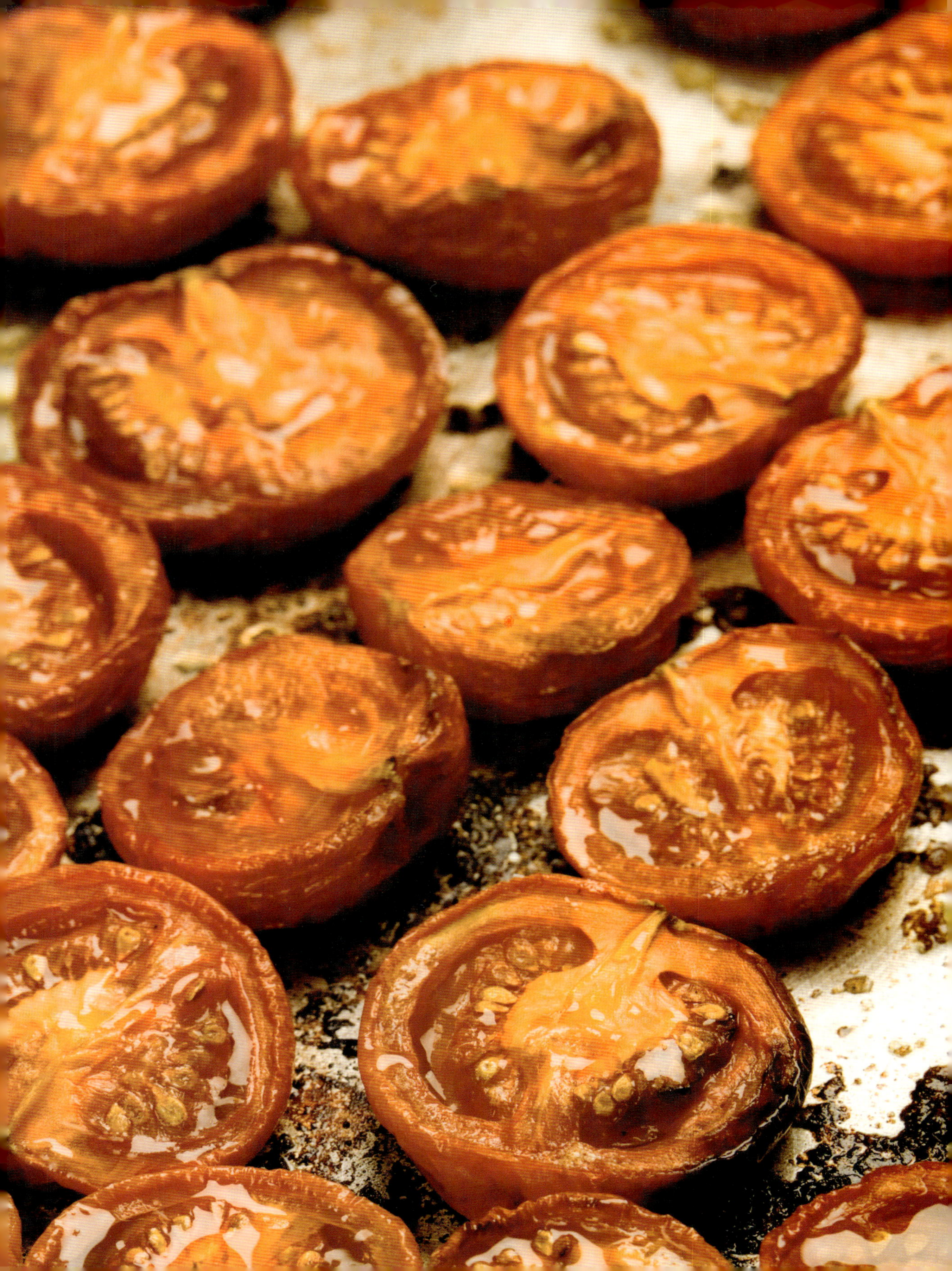

Pestos

Pestos are extremely versatile. In fact, you can make them depending on what ingredients you have in the cupboard. They are also quick to make and can be used in many different ways. But what is especially great for busy families is that pesto can make a substantial and easy meal very quickly. The most obvious use for pesto is in pasta dishes, but why not try livening up soups, using it on pizzas, making pesto croutons or mixing it with breadcrumbs to make a pesto crust? You could also drizzle it on vegetable tarts to add flavour, or stuff mushrooms or other vegetables with it.

Here are some different pesto recipes, but these are very adaptable so feel free to experiment with these ideas (and you'll find a few more at the end). Some of these recipes involve pine nuts. If you have time, roast them in a pan, under the grill or in an oven for five minutes as this will really heighten the flavour of the pesto. There are no serving sizes, because pesto can be used in so many different ways, but if you don't use all of your pesto in one go, cover it in olive oil and keep it in the fridge for up to five days. Just make sure that you bring it up to room temperature before stirring it into pasta dishes.

V, GF, N

Pistachio, cashew, rocket and basil pesto (makes approximately 300ml)

2 cloves of garlic – peeled
30g rocket
15g fresh basil leaves
100ml extra virgin olive oil
50ml vegetable oil
salt and pepper
50g pistachio nuts, shelled
50g cashew nuts

Preheat the oven to 180°C/gas mark 4. Place the garlic, rocket, basil, vegetable oil and olive oil in a bowl and half-blend using a hand blender (use a food processor or bar blender if you haven't got a hand blender). Add salt and pepper to taste.

Spread the pistachio nuts on a roasting tray and put them into the oven for 3–4 minutes. Roast the cashew nuts for about 5–6 minutes at the same temperature; they may need a stir after about 3–4 minutes to prevent them catching.

Take the nuts out of the oven as soon as they start to change colour and become dark brown. Add them to the rest of the ingredients and blend them in. The pesto should not be too smooth; it should still retain some texture.

V, GF, N

Sun-dried tomato, black olive, basil and pine-nut pesto (makes approximately 300ml)

2 cloves of garlic, peeled
100g pitted black olives
150g sun-dried tomatoes (rehydrated)
half a medium bunch of basil, leaves only
5 tbsp extra virgin olive oil
5 tbsp vegetable oil
50g roasted pine nuts
salt and pepper

Put all the ingredients in a food processor or liquidiser and blend them well for at least 2 minutes. Add salt and pepper to taste.

If you buy sun-dried tomatoes in oil, you won't need to rehydrate them. However dry sun-dried tomatoes will keep for longer and are far more cost effective, but they will be too tough to eat and almost without flavour until you rehydrate them. This is easy to do. Place the dry sun-dried tomatoes in a pan, add cold water, cover and bring to the boil. Take the pan off the heat as soon as the water comes to the boil and leave it for 30 minutes, before draining the tomatoes well.

GF

Basil, vegetarian parmesan and lemon thyme pesto (makes approximately 300ml)

There is no such thing as vegetarian parmesan. In the restaurant we use a fantastic English parmesan-style hard cheese.

half a large bunch of fresh basil, leaves only
half a large bunch of lemon thyme, leaves only
150g vegetarian parmesan-style cheese, grated
100ml extra virgin olive oil
salt and pepper

Put all the ingredients in a blender and half-blend them. Check for seasoning and add salt and pepper as required.

V, N, GF

Basil, rocket and pine-nut pesto (makes approximately 200ml)

4 tbsp vegetable oil
3 tbsp olive oil
2 cloves of garlic
100g rocket
60g pine nuts
1 tsp salt
half a small bunch of basil, leaves only

Put all the ingredients in a blender and half-blend them.

Some ideas for using pesto

Tomato, mozzarella and pesto tart

Just cut a 10cm square of ready-made puff pastry, top it with a slice of tomato, a slice of mozzarella and a spoonful of your favourite pesto, then put it in an oven preheated to 180°C/gas mark 4 for 10–15 minutes.

VO

Pesto and ricotta-stuffed mushrooms

Mix 80g breadcrumbs into 1 tbsp of your favourite pesto. Use this to stuff 4 medium portabello mushrooms, adding a spoonful of ricotta first, if desired. Pop them into a 180°C/gas mark 4 oven for 20 minutes.

Dressings

Dressings are very important in vegetarian cooking as they are used not only for salads but also for vegetables, cheese and nuts, adding another dimension and flavour to a dish. In the restaurant we do not use any genetically modified foods, and this includes our oils. Some oils such as vegetable oil are used as texture whereas other oils, such as walnut, rapeseed or extra virgin olive oil, are used to add specific flavours. Using the wrong type of oil can give a dressing an overpowering or bitter aftertaste.

The mirin dressing is used in our tofu pocket recipe on page 102. Mirin is a Japanese sweet rice wine that is widely available in good supermarkets. Tamari is a gluten-free soy sauce so if you don't need a gluten-free one any good soy sauce can be used.

The mango dressing is for our warm halloumi, wasabi-cashew, mango and avocado salad (page 18). The mango purée used in the dressing can be bought in tins or frozen and is used in preference to fresh mango for its concentrated flavour. All these dressings are based on 6 servings.

V, GF, S
Mirin dressing

4 tbsp mirin
1 tbsp vegetable oil
2 tbsp sesame oil
1 tbsp caster sugar
3 tbsp tamari
2 tbsp white wine

Place all the ingredients in a bowl and whisk them together.

V, GF
Lemon and coriander dressing

juice of 2 lemons
1 tbsp rapeseed or extra virgin olive oil
3 tbsp vegetable oil
1 medium bunch of coriander
1 tbsp caster sugar

Put all the ingredients in a blender and blend them together.

V, GF
Balsamic dressing

4 tbsp balsamic vinegar
5 tbsp olive oil
1 tbsp brown sugar

Whisk the ingredients together in a bowl, using a hand whisk.

V, GF
Mango dressing

2 lemon grass stalks, topped and tailed
half a red chilli, deseeded, and sliced in half again
1 clove of garlic
5 tbsp mango purée
2 tbsp water

Bash the lemon grass stalks and split them lengthways to release their flavour. Place all the ingredients in a small saucepan and gently bring to the boil, stirring regularly. Cook for 7 minutes and drain through a fine colander. Allow to cool before use.

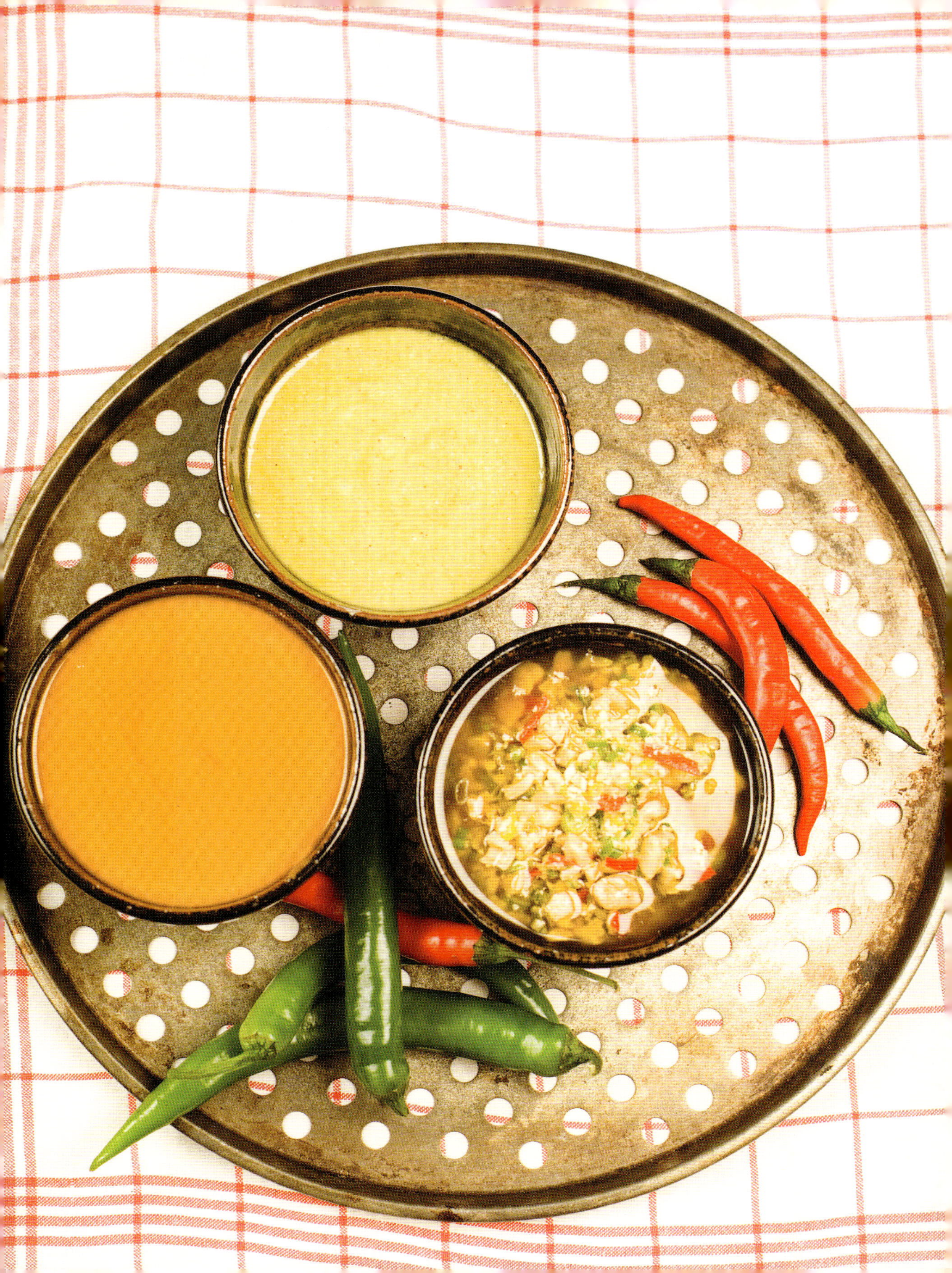

Flavoured oils

Home-made flavoured oils are very easy to make and really add that little extra flavour to the most simple of dishes: for example, steamed fine green beans or mashed potato can become amazingly delicious with a drizzle of garlic oil. Adding flavoured oils to salad dressings, mayonnaise or when making breads can really add interest. In our kitchen there are always garlic and chilli oil to hand. The shelf-life for oils tends to be shorter than it is for most preserves – they lose some of their flavour about four months after being opened.

It is really important to use sterilised bottles and closures. Bottles can be sterilised in several ways, but it's easiest to either run them through a dishwasher on a hot cycle or wash and rinse them and then allow them to dry in a very low oven. Do this shortly before you want to use them, and make sure they are really dry. Closures need to be sterilised too. Corks should be new and boiled for 10 minutes or kept submerged in boiling water for 15 minutes before use, which has an additional benefit: it makes them easier to push into the bottle. Screw tops and twist-on lids can also be sterilised in this way.

V, GF
Rosemary and garlic oil

20 cloves of garlic
600ml olive (ideally extra virgin) or sunflower oil
1 medium bunch of rosemary

Preheat the oven to 180°C/gas mark 4. Place the garlic in a roasting tin and roast it in the oven for about 5 minutes (you can keep the skins on). Put the oil in a pan, add the roasted garlic and rosemary and simmer over a low heat for about 5 minutes. Take the pan off the heat and let the oil cool for a further 5 minutes. Then pour it into a sterilised bottle and seal with a sterilised lid or cork. Leave it in a sunny place for one week, occasionally shaking the bottle. After this, strain the oil through a double thickness of muslin into a freshly sterilised bottle; you can add a sprig of rosemary to the oil if you like. Seal with a freshly sterilised lid.

V, GF
Lemon grass and chilli oil

Until the stalk has been crushed, the fragrance of lemon grass is actually quite mild. This lemony smell is a distinctive element in a lot of South East Asian cooking. To use fresh lemon grass, peel away and discard the fibrous outer layer, then pound the inner stalks using a pestle and mortar.

4 medium red chillies, with seeds
600ml olive (ideally extra virgin) or rapeseed oil
4 lemon grass stalks, peeled and pounded

Cut the chillies in half lengthways. Put them in a pan with the oil and lemon grass, bring it to a gentle simmer and cook, uncovered, at a relaxed bubble for 20 minutes. Decant into a sterilised jar or bottle and seal. Then leave it in a sunny place for about a week. Strain the oil through a double thickness of muslin into a newly sterilised bottle and seal as before, using a freshly sterilised cork or lid.

Marinating olives

We often experiment with different marinades for olives as it is a great way to pep them up and make them quite special. They are great to serve at the beginning of a dinner party with drinks as your guests arrive and you could make these little fellas the day before and allow to marinate overnight.

Marinated olives will last up to a week in an airtight container in the fridge. If you want to keep them for longer then use a sterilised jar with a lid, add the olives and then completely fill the jar with olive oil and make sure there are no air pockets around the olives. The olives can be kept like this in the fridge for up to a month.

Here are several flavouring options. In all cases, make them in the same way: combine the ingredients in a bowl, and allow them to marinate overnight in the fridge.

V, GF

Black olives in lemon and rosemary

150–200g black olives

half a preserved lemon, finely sliced with its juice

1 tbsp rosemary, finely chopped

3 tbsp olive oil

V, GF

Green olives in fresh herbs, lemon and chilli

150g green olives

3 tbsp olive oil

2 cloves of garlic, finely chopped

2 tbsp fresh parsley, chopped

1 tbsp fresh basil, finely chopped

2 tbsp lemon juice

½ tsp chilli flakes

V, GF

Green olives marinated in orange zest, mint and cumin

150g green olives

zest of 1 orange, finely diced

1 tbsp mint leaves, chopped

1 tbsp cumin

2 cloves of garlic, finely chopped

3 tbsp olive oil

V, GF

Black olives with roasted red pepper and capers

150g black olives

1 roasted red pepper, deseeded and finely chopped

½ tbsp capers, finely chopped

1 tbsp fresh basil, finely chopped

3 tbsp olive oil

1 tsp balsamic vinegar

Toasted seeds and nuts

There are two different methods you can use for toasting seeds and nuts. The first is to use a dry frying pan over a medium heat, the other is to put them on a baking tray and roast them in a medium to hot oven, on the top shelf. However there are a couple of rules: never use any oil or butter as it will make the seeds or nuts go soft, and never take your eyes off them as they will heat and cook very quickly. Just before nuts and seeds are cooked through, they will darken slightly, so take them off the heat or out of the oven immediately as they will carry on cooking for a little on their own.

For the oven method, preheat the oven to 180°C/gas mark 4.

V, GF, N
Mixed roasted nuts, with sultanas and orange-peel chilli

Shichimi powder is an orange Japanese chilli powder with black sesame seeds in it which can be bought online or in Oriental supermarkets.

65g cashews
65g almonds
125g sultanas
250g sunflower seeds, toasted
250g peanuts, unsalted
2 tbsp shichimi powder

Roast the cashews and the almonds for three minutes in the oven until golden brown. Mix with the other ingredients, allow to cool and store in a sterilised airtight jar.

V, GF
Tamarind-coated mixed seeds

250g sunflower seeds
250g pumpkin seeds
2 tbsp tamarind paste

Mix the seeds with the tamarind paste and then roast them on a baking tray in the oven for 10 minutes, watching to make sure they don't burn; give the tray a shake every so often. Store in an airtight jar.

V, GF, N
Roasted wasabi cashew nuts

300g cashew nuts
1 tbsp wasabi paste

Toss the cashew nuts in the wasabi paste (if you like hot foods, then add a little more). Put a piece of baking paper on an oven tray and scatter the cashews over it. Roast them in the oven for 5 minutes, then shake the tray and cook for another 5 minutes. Allow them to cool on the baking paper and then store in an airtight jar.

GF, VO, N
Honey-glazed walnuts

300g walnuts
2 tbsp runny honey

Place a piece of baking paper on an oven tray and put the walnuts on it. Roast them in the oven for 10 minutes. As they come out, drizzle them with the honey and then allow them to cool and set.

If you don't want to use honey, then the walnuts can be glazed by heating 2 tablespoons of caster sugar or maple syrup in a frying pan over a gentle heat, so that it melts into a syrup. Then toss the walnuts in this syrup, turn them out onto some baking paper and allow them to cool.

N
Roasted pine nuts

We use pine nuts in several of our recipes and they always taste better when they have been toasted first. Place them on a tray and put it in the oven for 10 minutes. If you are in a rush you can place them under a medium grill, but you cannot look away as they will burn very easily.

Jams and preserves

At the end of the summer in the Food for Friends kitchen, the competition heightens between the chefs to see who can make the best batches of chutneys and jams. Here are some of our favourite recipes from our kitchen. The pear and plum chutney and spiced, pickled pears are used with our patés and terrines. The chilli jam is very versatile and is used with our cheese scones, burgers and Thai platters.

V, GF
Chilli jam

Makes one large jar

1 x 400g tin of tomatoes
300g sugar
3 tbsp lemon juice
5 tbsp white wine vinegar
4–8 red chillies (to taste), deseeded
1 ½ tsp salt

Put all the ingredients in a saucepan. Simmer on a low heat until the mixture becomes really thick, which should take approximately 20 minutes. Pour it into warmed sterile jars and seal, making sure the jars are airtight. This jam will keep for up to six months unopened; once opened, use within a month and keep refrigerated.

V, GF
Pear and plum chutney

This chutney is simple to make and really useful; we serve it with our patés.
But it is also delicious when served as part of a cheeseboard, with fresh bread.

Makes one large jar

1 tbsp vegetable oil
200g red onions, finely sliced
1 tsp salt
1 tsp mixed spice
1 ½ tsp fennel seeds
1 ½ tsp mustard seeds
1 tsp ground coriander
190ml white wine vinegar
250g caster sugar
3 pears, peeled, cored and diced
300g plums, stoned and cut into roughly eight pieces each

Take the fennel, mustard, ground coriander and mixed spice and gently dry fry them on a low heat in a non-stick pan for 10 minutes, stirring continuously. This will help to release more of the flavours.

Put the oil in a large pan, and gently fry the red onions over a low heat for 10 minutes so they become very soft. Then add the rest of the ingredients except the pears and plums, and turn the heat up to allow the sugar to dissolve.

When the mixture starts to boil, turn the heat down again. Add the fruit and mix well. Simmer on a low heat for 40 minutes to allow the fruit to cook through. Transfer into sterile jars and seal them with greaseproof paper and sterile lids.

V, GF
Spiced pickled pears
Serves 6

6 hard pears (Conference or similar)
100g soft brown sugar
350ml cider vinegar
1 tbsp balsamic vinegar
1 tbsp whole mixed peppercorns
4 whole cloves
6 juniper berries
4 star anise
4 cinammon

Preheat the oven to 190°C/gas mark 5.

Peel the pears but leave the stalks intact as they look prettier, then slice them into halves. Place all the rest of the ingredients in a heatproof casserole over a steady heat and bring to a simmering point, stirring all the time to dissolve the sugar. Carefully lower the pears into the liquid, lying them on their sides.

Cover the casserole with a lid and transfer it to the oven for 30 minutes. Then take it out, turn the pears over and replace the casserole in the oven; the pears should need another 30 minutes to be soft, but check during cooking. Store in a sterile airtight jar.

Papaya and avocado salad with a cashew and chilli dressing, page 19

Salads

VO, GF, N
Warm haloumi, wasabi-cashew nut, mango and avocado salad

This salad has evolved on our menu over the last few years but has remained a firm favourite with both regulars and new customers alike. What's great is that it's a salad which can be adapted to suit everyone. It is naturally gluten-free and low in fat, is easily made vegan – by replacing the halloumi with grilled or pan-fried tofu pieces – and it tastes delicious. Halloumi is originally from Cyprus but in the restaurant we use a delicious organic English variety from a local Sussex farm. All varieties of halloumi have a chewy texture and salty flavour, which is why they tend to be griddled or pan-fried and eaten straightaway.

Serves 4

100g unsalted cashew nuts
½ tsp wasabi paste
2 ripe medium mangoes
1 ripe large avocado
250g packet of mixed baby salad leaves
1 portion of mango dressing (see page 8)
400g Cypriot haloumi

Preheat the oven to 180°C/gas mark 4 and mix the cashews with the wasabi paste. Put the cashews on a baking tray and roast them in the oven for 10 minutes. Allow them to cool.

Dice the mango, and then the avocado. Place the salad leaves in a large bowl. Set 2 tablespoons of the mango dressing to one side and pour the rest over the leaves. Toss the salad, and then mix in the mango and avocado pieces. Put the salad leaves onto individual plates and sprinkle the wasabi cashew nuts over the top.

Oil a griddle pan and put it over a high heat. Cut the haloumi into thick slices and cook it on the griddle for two minutes on each side, then arrange on top of the salad. Drizzle the remaining mango dressing around the plates. Serve immediately.

V, GF, N, S

Papaya and avocado salad with a cashew nut and chilli dressing

This is a really pretty salad that would work well as a starter for a dinner or lunch party.

Serves 4

2 ripe papaya
1 ripe avocado
juice of 1 lime
half a cucumber, peeled
1 carrot, peeled
1 stick of celery
1 bunch of spring onions, tops only (the green bits – save the rest for the dressing)
coriander leaves, to garnish

For the dressing:
100g cashew nuts, chopped with a knife
2 limes – the zest of one and the juice of two
1 medium red chilli, deseeded and very finely diced (2mm)
1 tbsp sesame oil
2 tbsp extra virgin olive oil
1 bunch of spring onions, the bottom white part, chopped finely
salt and pepper
1 clove of garlic, finely chopped

Peel and deseed the papaya, then dice it into 6mm cubes. Do the same with the avocado, but place the pieces in a bowl. Squeeze some lime juice over them and add the avocado stone to the bowl; this should stop the avocado from discolouring. Take the cucumber, remove the seeds in the middle and chop it into 6mm cubes.

Cut the carrot, celery and spring onion tops into fine strips about 2mm wide and place them in a bowl of iced water until you are ready to serve the salad.

Put all the dressing ingredients in a bowl and whisk them together thoroughly. Add the diced papaya, avocado and cucumber to the dressing, and mix well. Place a 9cm diameter ring (or one of whatever size you would like your salad to be) on the centre of each plate. Using a slotted spoon, spoon the papaya, avocado and cucumber mix into the ring and press it down with the back of the spoon. Carefully remove the ring.

Take a little handful of the carrot, spring onion and celery ribbons and shake off the water. Shape them into a ball in your hands and carefully place on top of the salad.

Drizzle some dressing over and around the salad; garnish with coriander leaves.

GF, S, N
Warm asparagus, artichoke and marinated roasted aubergine salad with honey walnuts and a tahini dressing

This is a lovely summer salad that we like to serve as a casual lunch in a big bowl where everyone can dig in and help themselves. It is really a meal in itself, but you could serve it at a barbeque, or perhaps with some lovely home-made focaccia and a chilled glass of white wine…

Serves 6

4 tbsp olive oil
6 medium vine tomatoes
salt and pepper
100g walnut halves
3 tbsp runny honey
2 large aubergines, cut lengthways into 2cm slices
400g asparagus spears, bottoms trimmed
400g long-stemmed artichokes marinated in oil
6 small figs
25g butter
2 tbsp caster sugar
400g bag of mixed baby leaf salad

For the aubergines' marinade:
1 clove of garlic, peeled
sea salt
4 sprigs of fresh thyme
3 tbsp olive oil
3 tbsp sunflower oil
1 tbsp fresh parsley, finely chopped

For the salad dressing:
juice of 1 lemon
5 tbsp olive oil
sea salt
2 tsp tahini
a handful of coriander leaves (stalks removed)
2 tbsp sunflower oil

Preheat the oven to 180°C/gas mark 4 and pour the oil into a shallow dish. Put the tomatoes in an oven tray, drizzle with a little olive oil and sprinkle with sea salt and freshly ground pepper. Place in the oven for 15–20 minutes or until they are soft and bursting out of their skins.

Spread the walnut halves in another baking tray, drizzle them with honey and then put them in the oven for 5 minutes. Take them out and put them on a piece of greaseproof paper, separating the walnut pieces so they do not stick together.

To make the marinade for the aubergines, finely chop the clove of garlic, then sprinkle it with salt. Using the flat of the knife, mash the garlic and salt together to form a paste. Put it in a large bowl. Pull the leaves off the sprigs of thyme and put them in the bowl too, then add the two oils and the parsley. Mix everything together and set to one side.

Heat a lightly oiled griddle pan on the hob. Take the slices of aubergine and dip both sides in the bowl of olive oil. When the griddle is hot enough – it will begin to smoke – place the aubergine slices on it. Cook for 5 minutes on each side, or until the aubergines are soft and nicely chargrilled on either side. Cut each of the aubergine slices into four chunks and allow them to cool for a few minutes. Then put the chunks of aubergine into the marinade and leave for 30 minutes.

Bring a small pan of water to the boil. Cook the asparagus for three minutes, then plunge it into a bowl of iced water, then out again, and set it aside too. Blend all the salad dressing ingredients together and put that to one side as well.

When the aubergines have been marinating for 25 minutes, reheat the griddle. Now place the artichoke hearts on the griddle for a minute on each side and sprinkle them with a little black pepper. Remove them from the griddle and keep them warm. Chargrill the asparagus spears for a minute either side.

Finally take the figs, cut off the stalks and cut them in half through the top. Melt the butter in a small frying pan, then add the sugar and allow it to dissolve. Place the fig halves in the pan flat side down and allow them to cook for 3 minutes, then turn them over and cook for one more minute. Take off the heat and set aside.

To assemble the salad, mix the salad leaves and the aubergine pieces, drained from their marinade, in a large bowl. Add the dressing and mix well. Turn out onto a large serving plate or shallow bowl and add the figs, tomatoes, artichokes, asparagus and walnut pieces. Serve immediately.

N, GFO
Sautéed wild mushroom, poached pear and walnut salad with a creamy dolcelatte and truffle oil dressing, served with crostini

This is an elegant salad which is really jam-packed with lots of different but complementing flavours and our take on the classic pear and dolcelatte flavour combination. Most wild mushrooms in England come into season during the autumn though you can use morels in early spring.

Serves 4

For the pears:
1 litre water
5 star anise
10 whole cloves
4 small cinnamon sticks
80g sugar
4 Conference or William pears, peeled, cored and cut into quarters lengthways

For the mushrooms:
2 tbsp vegetable oil
400g mixed wild mushrooms, such as oyster, shiitake, trompette, girolle, cep, cut or pulled apart

For the walnuts:
100g walnuts
1½ tbsp runny honey

For the crostini:
8 slices of stale Italian bread (focaccia or ciabatta)
a little olive oil
One large bag of mixed salad leaves

For the salad dressing:
2 tbsp extra virgin olive oil
4 tbsp balsamic vinegar
2 tsp truffle oil
2 tsp walnut oil
salt and pepper

For the dolcelatte dressing:
3 tbsp extra virgin olive oil
2 tbsp vegetable oil
1 clove of garlic, crushed
salt and pepper
100g dolcelatte

Preheat the oven to 180°C/gas mark 4. Pour the water into a large pan and add the star anise, cloves, cinnamon sticks and sugar. Bring to the boil. Add the pears and allow to cook for a further 5 minutes. Remove from the heat and leave to cool. Keep the pears in the syrup and refrigerate until you are ready to use them.

Sauté the mushrooms in two tablespoons of vegetable oil until soft. Do not season or add butter to them.

Place the walnuts on a piece of baking paper on an oven tray and roast them in the oven for 6–7 minutes until golden in colour. Place them in a bowl as soon as you take them out of the oven and stir in the runny honey, and then return them to the baking paper, spreading them out so they don't stick together as they cool.

To make the crostini lower the oven temperature to 130°C/gas mark ½. Put the slices of bread on a baking sheet, drizzle with olive oil and then dry them in the oven for 5–7 minutes.

Put the salad leaves in a large bowl and make the dressing. Mix the olive oil, balsamic vinegar, truffle oil and walnut oil together, check the seasoning, and then toss it with the leaves. Divide the salad between the plates.

For the dolcelatte dressing, blend the olive oil with the vegetable oil, garlic and some salt and pepper. Then add the dolcelatte and blend for one minute only, otherwise it will split. It should be a smooth creamy sauce.

Divide the mushrooms, pears and walnuts between the plates, putting them on top of the leaves. The dolcelatte dressing and the bread should be served next to the leaves.

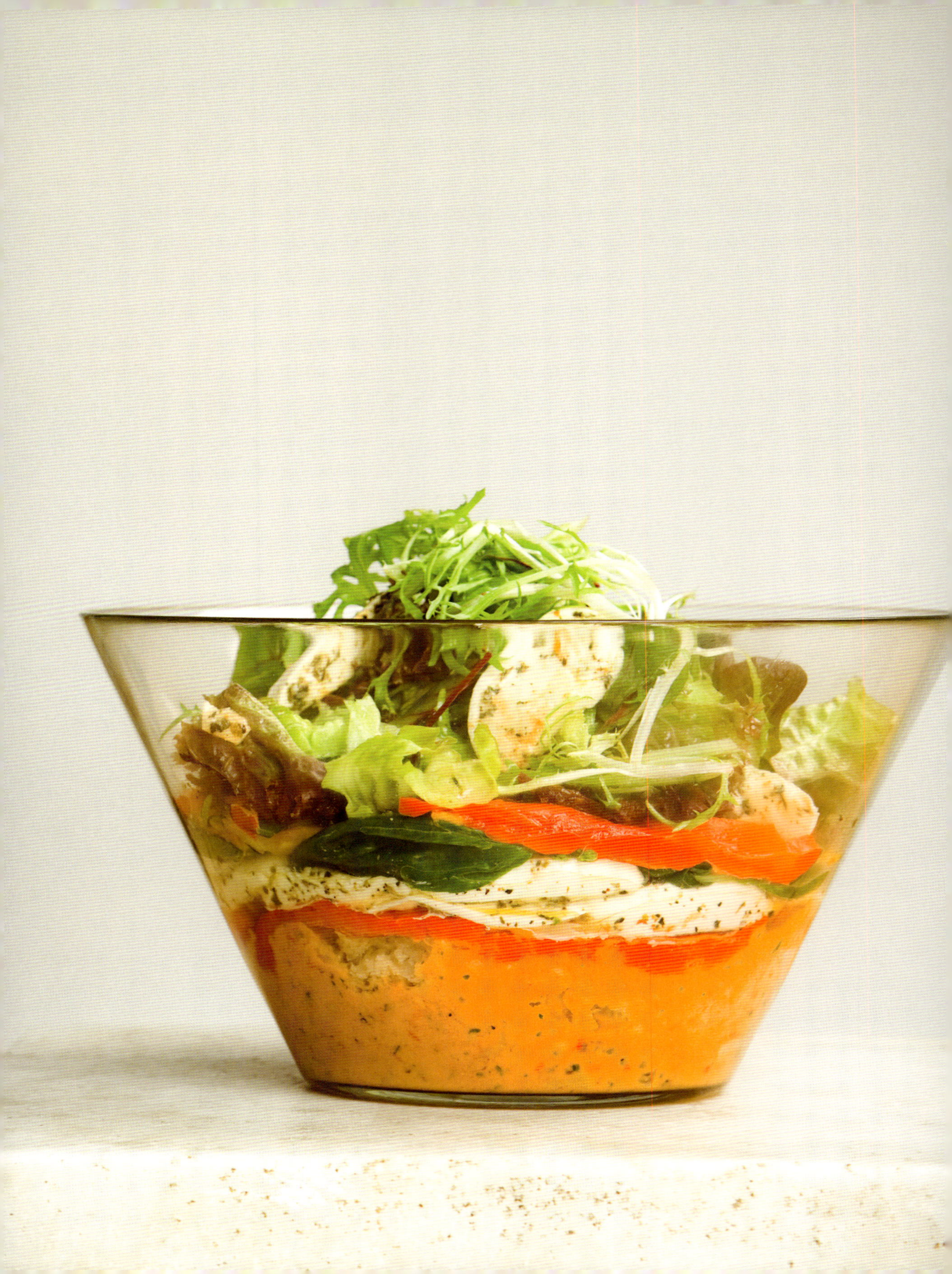

VO, GFO
Panzanella salad with roast vegetables

There are various ways of serving this dish. It is a beautiful salad to look at, and our favourite way is to serve it in a large glass bowl so you are able to see all the layers – it is great for parties. If you want to make it more of a meal, then you can put a layer of couscous at the bottom before layering in the salad; otherwise you can make sculpted salads on individual plates, up to you… To make this dish vegan, don't add the mozzarella; it's not essential, but it does provide a different colour when layering the salad. For a gluten-free option, use gluten-free bread.

Serves 8–10

- 5 yellow peppers
- 5 red peppers
- a little olive oil (for roasting peppers)
- 3 large red onions, each cut into eight segments
- 500g stale Italian bread, cut into chunky cubes
- 4 large beef tomatoes
- 2 large white onions, roughly chopped
- 1 medium bunch of chives, chopped
- 1 medium bunch of basil, chopped (but leave some whole)
- 170ml extra virgin olive oil
- 300ml sunflower oil
- 2 cloves of garlic
- 50ml balsamic vinegar
- salt and pepper
- 500g buffalo mozzarella
- 450g cherry tomatoes, skinned if possible
- a handful of pitted black olives
- 1 bag of mixed baby salad leaves
- 40g caper berries
- 1 bunch of basil leaves, stalks removed

Preheat the oven to 200°C/gas mark 6. Slice the stalk ends from the peppers and then scoop out the white parts in the middle and the seeds. Rub them with olive oil and place on an oven tray. Place in the oven for 20 minutes to roast. Put the red onion segments in another roasting tray, drizzle them with olive oil and salt, and roast them for 10–15 minutes or until coloured and soft. Put the chunks of bread on a baking tray, drizzle them with olive oil too and roast them in the oven for 10 minutes.

Chop the beef tomatoes into cubes and place in a large bowl. Add the chopped white onion and herbs, the two oils, the garlic and the vinegar. Using a hand blender, create a smooth sauce (they can also be pulsed in a food processor). Season with salt and pepper, and stir this sauce over the bread when it comes out of the oven.

When the peppers have cooled down, peel the skin off and cut them into quarters. If you are using mozzarella, cut it into cubes.

Assemble the salad. Take a large tall bowl or individual ones and layer the peppers, mozzarella, bread, cherry tomatoes, roasted red onions, black olives and whole basil leaves. Then scatter the salad leaves and a few caper berries on top, and serve immediately to stop the leaves wilting.

V, GF, N
Thai pomelo and star fruit salad with a chilli and lime dressing

This salad is really fresh and good for a detox. It is popular in Southeast Asia, where the pomelo is a native citrus fruit. If you can't find a pomelo – try Oriental supermarkets – then you can substitute a pink grapefruit, but it is worth searching. Whatever you use, you must eat the salad straight after it's been tossed in the dressing, as this is when the flavour really intensifies – it goes into a steady decline afterwards. So forget leaving some for later, it needs to be eaten immediately!

Serves 4

- a quarter of a white cabbage, shredded (optional)
- 1 pomelo, peeled, de-pithed and cut into segments
- 200g bean sprouts
- 3 juicy tomatoes, cut into small wedges
- 1 star fruit, thinly sliced
- 1 small bunch of coriander, leaves finely chopped
- 6 large mint leaves, finely chopped
- 3 tbsp chopped peanuts

For the dressing:
- 1 red chilli, deseeded and chopped
- 2 limes, juice and zest
- 2 tbsp lemon juice
- 1 clove of garlic, peeled
- 20g fresh ginger, peeled and roughly chopped
- 2 tbsp sesame oil
- 1 tbsp white wine vinegar
- 100ml extra virgin olive oil
- salt and pepper

First make the dressing, as the key is freshness. Put all the dressing ingredients into a blender and blend them together to make a smooth dressing. Set it aside.

Mix the white cabbage, the pomelo segments, bean sprouts, tomatoes and star fruit slices in a bowl.

Add the dressing, the chopped coriander and mint leaves to the bowl and toss the salad well. Divide it between individual plates if you wish and sprinkle the chopped peanuts over the top. Serve immediately.

GFO
Watercress, orange, grapefruit and dolcelatte salad

This is a delicious, light salad that could be eaten on its own or as an accompaniment to one of the fritter or wellington recipes further on in the book. Try to use pink peppercorns that have been preserved in oil as they are lovely and soft. Originally from Brazil, these peppercorns are actually the dried fruit of the Baies Rose. They have a sweet, peppery flavour and look very pretty in dishes.

Serves 6

1 orange
2 pink or white grapefruit
2 tablespoons olive oil
salt and pepper
250g watercress, tough stems discarded
2 tsp pink peppercorns, preserved in oil
6 slices rye or gluten-free bread
200g vegetarian blue cheese, crumbled (we use dolcelatte as it is gluten-free and vegetarian)

Remove the skin and pith from the orange and the grapefruit and cut them into segments – do this over a bowl so the juices are retained. Whisk the olive oil and two tablespoons of the citrus juices together in a large bowl; add a little seasoning. Then add the watercress, fruit segments and the pink peppercorns. Toss everything together.

Grill or toast the rye bread and cut it into triangles.

Divide the salad onto plates, scatter it with the crumbled cheese and serve with the toasted rye triangles.

Beetroot soup with a spinach and feta salsa, page 30

Soups

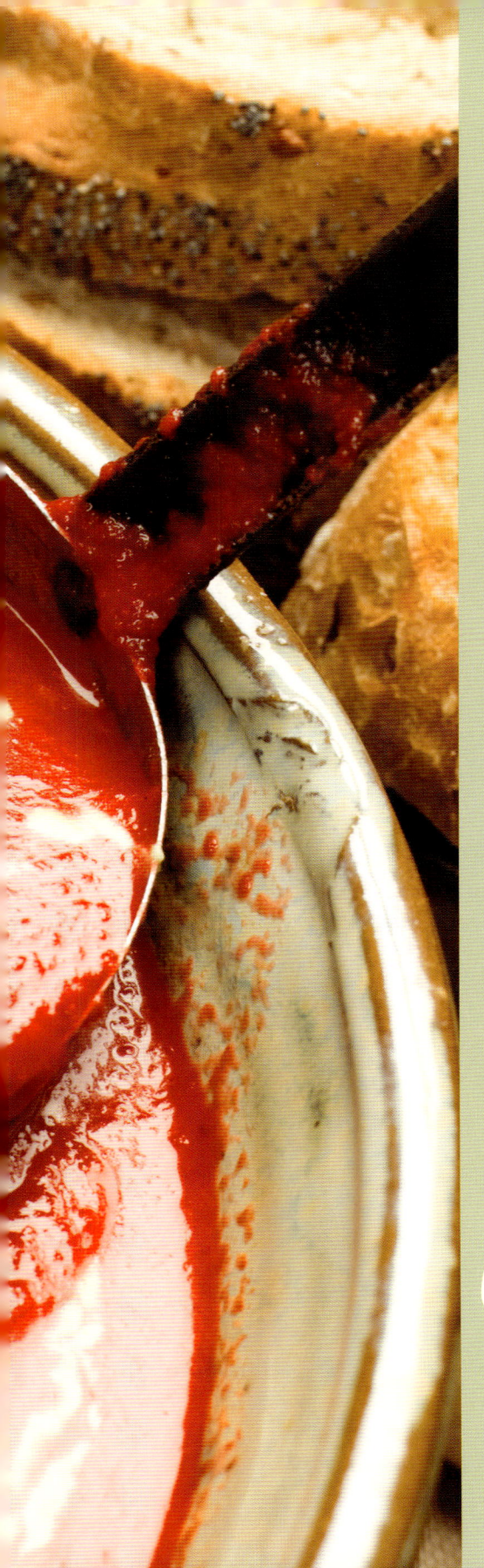

Beetroot soup with a spinach and feta salsa

GF

This soup is a stunner. The colour is really rather voluptuous and it is great either as a chilled summer soup or served warm in colder months. If you want to serve it warm, make the salsa first; otherwise you can do that as the soup cools down.

Serves 6

400ml vegetarian red wine
150g caster sugar
2 tbsp vegetable oil
3 red onions, finely chopped
4 cloves of garlic, finely chopped
3 sticks of celery, finely chopped
1kg fresh beetroot, washed, peeled and diced
3 litres vegetable stock
salt and pepper

For the feta and spinach salsa:
100g fresh baby spinach
200g Greek feta cheese, roughly chopped
1 clove of garlic, finely chopped
2 tbsp double cream
black pepper

Put the wine in a small saucepan and stir in the sugar. Simmer gently until the wine has turned into a thick syrup – it should reduce by a little more than half the original amount. Set the pan aside.

Put the oil in a large thick-based saucepan and sweat the onions, garlic and celery for 10 minutes; make sure they do not brown. Then add the diced beetroot and vegetable stock, and pour in the wine reduction. Season with salt and pepper. Cook for 20–30 minutes until the beetroot is soft. Using a hand blender or food processor, blend the soup to a smooth consistency. If you are serving it cold, set it to one side to cool before chilling in the refrigerator.

To make the salsa, blanch the spinach in boiling water for 30 seconds, and immediately tip it into a sieve or colander. Squeeze the water out of the spinach either by hand or by pressing it with the back of a wooden spoon. Blend the feta, garlic and double cream together and season the resulting mixture with black pepper. Then add the spinach to the mix and blend everything together until it has a mousse-like consistency. When you are ready to serve the soup, whether it's hot or cold, swirl the salsa through it.

V, GF, S
Tom ka soup

This soup forms part of our Thai platter in the restaurant and is quite pungent, so not for the faint hearted. Although it can be served on its own it makes part of a great sharing platter served in espresso cups with the sweetcorn fritters and mango salad on page 87.

Serves 6

- 2 cloves of garlic
- 3 sticks of lemon grass, outer leaves and base removed
- 25g galangal (use ginger if galangal is not available)
- 1 red chilli, deseeded
- 1 small white onion
- 1 small bunch of coriander
- a little vegetable oil
- 30g green Thai curry paste
- 70ml water
- 1 vegetable stock cube
- 1 x 400ml tin coconut milk
- 1 tbsp tom ka paste
- 3 tbsp tamari (or a good soy sauce if gluten free is not required)
- 50g caster sugar
- 2 kaffir lime leaves
- juice of 1 lime
- a handful of coriander leaves, chopped
- a handful of cashew nuts, roughly chopped

Roughly chop the garlic, lemon grass, ginger, chilli, onion and coriander, including the coriander stalks. Heat a little oil in a pan, then add them to the pan and sweat them through for 5 minutes. Add the Thai curry paste and water, and crumble in the stock cube. Allow to simmer for 15 minutes.

Add the coconut milk and tom-ka paste, and continue to simmer for another 15 minutes. Then add the tamari, sugar, lime leaves and juice, and the chopped coriander leaves and mix everything well. Blend until smooth.

Serve the soup with the chopped cashew nuts scattered on top. You could also try adding some sliced spring onions and black sesame seeds to the cashews.

V, GF
Spiced pumpkin, sweet potato, coconut and ginger soup

Serves 4

1 tbsp vegan margarine
1 tbsp olive oil
2 large onions, thinly sliced
2 tbsp brown sugar
2 tsp coriander seeds
2 tsp whole cumin
600g pumpkin or butternut squash, peeled and chopped
2 sweet potatoes (approx. 450g), peeled and chopped
6cm piece of root ginger, peeled and chopped
2 x 400ml tins of light coconut milk

To garnish:
1 pink grapefruit
3 tbsp fresh coconut shavings
a few sprigs of coriander

Heat the butter and oil in a large pan and add the onions and sugar. Cook them gently for 15–20 minutes, stirring now and then, to soften and caramelise the onions. Meanwhile, toast the whole coriander and cumin in a small frying pan for about a minute or until they smell fragrant, then crush them finely using a pestle and mortar.

Add the toasted seeds, pumpkin or butternut squash, sweet potato, ginger and coconut milk to the pan with the caramelised onions. Fill one of the empty coconut milk tins with water and add that too. Bring the soup to a simmer, then reduce the heat and cook it slowly, partially covered, for about 15–20 minutes or until the vegetables are tender.

Purée the soup in batches, then return it to the pan. If the soup is too thick add a little water. Season to taste and reheat gently.

Remove the peel of the grapefruit, then slice the flesh. Top each bowl of soup with a slice of grapefruit, a little coconut and a few sprigs of coriander.

This soup can be frozen or kept chilled for up to two days.

GF
Spinach, lentil and lemon soup

This soup is very common across the Middle East. It is normally a winter dish, but is also often made as a restorative if someone is unwell.

Serves 6

3 tbsp oil
1 large onion, chopped
1 tbsp ground turmeric
100g yellow split peas
450g spinach, chopped
1.2 litres water
50g rice flour
juice of 2 lemons
salt and freshly ground black pepper
2 cloves of garlic
2 tbsp chopped fresh mint
4 eggs, beaten

Using a large frying pan, heat 2 tablespoons of the oil and fry the onion until golden. Add the turmeric, split peas, spinach and water and bring to the boil. Reduce the heat and simmer for 20 minutes.

Mix the rice flour with some more cold water (about 250ml) to make a smooth paste, and then slowly add it to the pan, stirring continuously to prevent lumps forming. Then stir in the lemon juice and season with salt and pepper. Cook gently for 20 minutes.

Meanwhile, heat the remaining tablespoon of oil in another pan and fry the garlic briefly until it is just golden. Stir in the mint and take the frying pan off the heat.

Remove the soup pan from the heat and stir in the beaten eggs. Sprinkle the garlic and mint on top of the soup and serve.

GF, N, VO
Chantenay carrot and butter bean soup with brazil nuts and thyme

This is good for the immune system and warding off colds! To make this dairy-free just use soya milk instead of the semi-skimmed milk.

Serves 4

- 1 tbsp olive oil or 15g butter
- 1 medium onion, chopped
- 2 cloves of garlic, chopped
- 500g Chantenay carrots
- 600ml vegetable stock (preferably fresh)
- 2 bay leaves
- 1 tbsp honey (manuka, if possible)
- 1 tbsp thyme leaves, plus a few extra
- 1 tbsp chopped coriander
- 1 medium parsnip, peeled and chopped into small cubes
- 1 x 410g tin butter beans, drained
- 300ml semi-skimmed or soya milk
- juice of 1 orange
- 2 tbsp chopped brazil nuts
- black pepper

Heat the oil or butter in a large non-stick pan or casserole and cook the onion for 4–5 minutes to allow it to soften. Add the garlic and cook for a further 2 minutes. Reserve 6 smaller carrots; trim and chop the rest and add them to the pan with the stock, bay, honey, thyme and coriander. Bring to the boil then simmer gently, covered, for 20 minutes or until the carrots are tender.

While the soup is cooking, trim and cut the reserved carrots into quarters, and mix them with the parsnip and butter beans.

Once the carrots in the pan are tender, take out the bay leaves and blend the soup in batches. Return it to the pan. Stir in the milk, quartered carrots, parsnips and butter beans. Simmer again, partially covered, for 15 minutes or until the vegetables are tender. Stir in the orange juice and warm the soup through briefly – don't allow it to come to the boil.

Sprinkle each serving of soup with a few chopped brazil nuts, some extra thyme leaves and a grinding of freshly ground black pepper.

V, GF
Chilled gazpacho

Gazpacho is a Spanish tomato-based raw vegetable soup which is usually served cold. There are many variations but this is the Food for Friends recipe…

Serves 4

½ cucumber, roughly chopped
3 sticks of celery, roughly chopped
1 red onion, peeled and coarsely chopped
4 cloves of garlic, peeled
1 red pepper, deseeded and roughly chopped
half a medium bunch of fresh oregano
half a medium bunch of parsley
3 tbsp red wine vinegar
10 ripe tomatoes
1 small red chilli, roughly chopped
100ml extra virgin olive oil
50ml water
1 tsp cumin
2 tsp smoked paprika
50g sugar
salt and pepper, to season

First peel the tomatoes. Score a cross on the bottom of each one and then plunge into boiling water for 5 seconds and then immediately into a bowl of iced water. The skin will now peel off easily.

Place all the ingredients in a large bowl and blend them to a smooth consistency using a hand blender, or put them all in a food processor and blend until smooth. Season with salt and pepper. Chill in the fridge for at least 3 hours and stir through before serving.

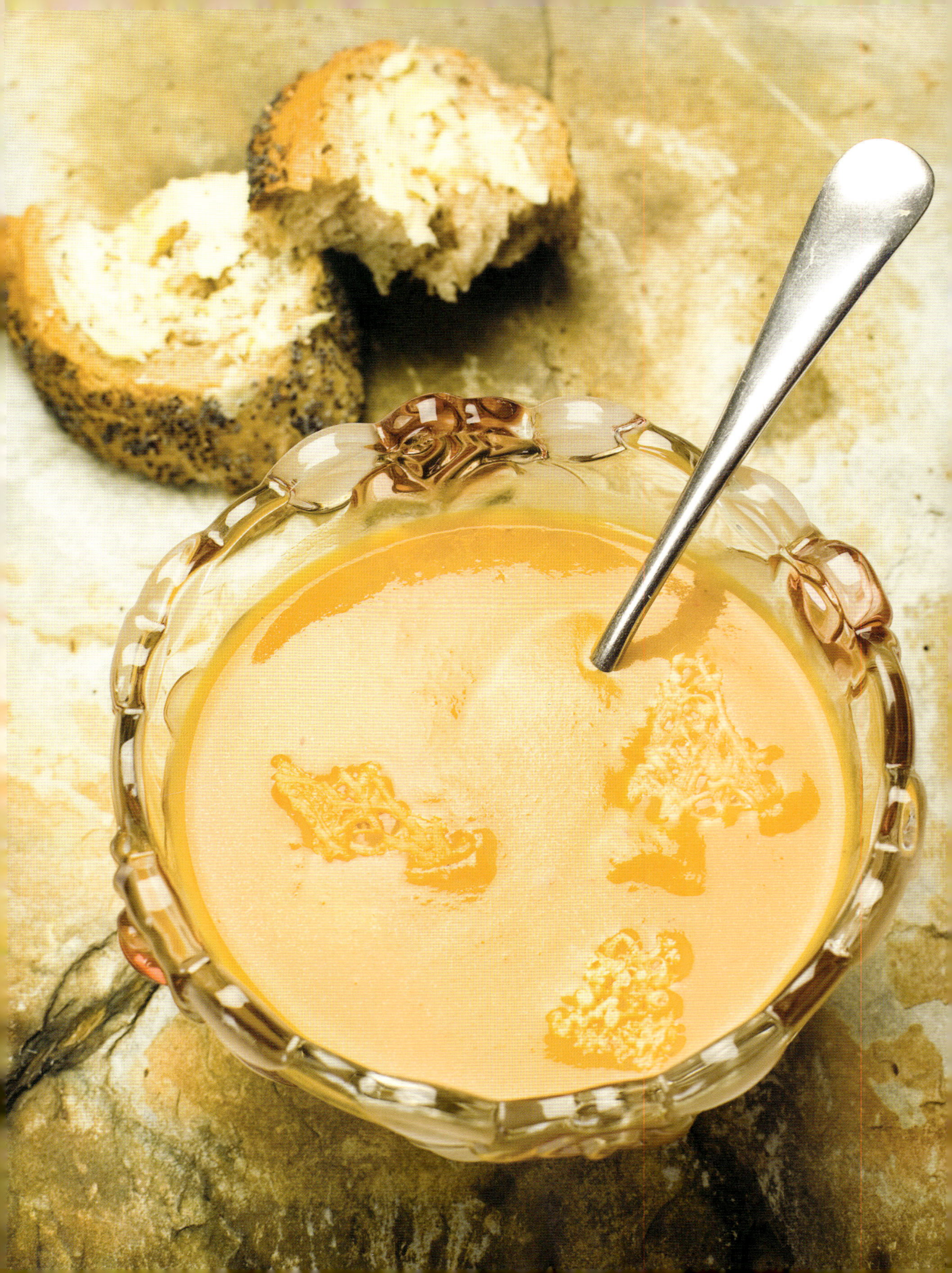

VO, GFO
Sweet potato and chestnut soup with cheesy crisps and crème fraîche

This delicious soup can be frozen, and the parmesan crisps will last up to two days. For a vegan option, omit the crème fraîche and the 'parmesan' crisps; to make it gluten-free, use gluten-free flour.

Serves 8–10

1kg sweet potato
2 leeks, peeled and finely sliced
a little vegetable oil
3 x 200g packs of vacuum-packed chestnuts
1 ½ litres vegetable stock
salt and pepper
1 whole nutmeg, for grating
1 tsp ground cumin
½ tsp paprika
1 x 200ml tub of crème fraîche

For the parmesan crisps:
50g grated parmesan-style vegetarian cheese
1 tbsp plain flour
black pepper

Preheat the oven to 180°C/gas mark 4. Peel the sweet potato and cut it into chunks. Sweat the leeks in a large saucepan with a little oil for 10 minutes until soft and golden, then add the sweet potato, 2 packets of the chestnuts, the stock and some seasoning. Bring to the boil, reduce the heat and partially cover the pan. Allow the soup to simmer gently for 30 minutes or until the vegetables are tender.

For the parmesan crisps, mix the parmesan and flour with some freshly ground pepper. Line a large baking sheet with some baking paper and put 8 small circles of cheese mixture on the baking paper, spacing them evenly. Bake for 7–8 minutes or until they have spread and are lightly golden. Cool them slightly, then peel off the paper and put the crisps on a wire rack to cool.

Remove the soup from the heat and allow it to cool a little. Then whiz it in a blender until smooth (do this in a couple of batches if necessary). Return the soup to the pan; if it is too thick, add a little water. Add the freshly grated nutmeg, the cumin and paprika and simmer for 10 minutes.

Chop up the last packet of chestnuts and set them aside. For serving, put the soup in individual bowls, add a spoonful of crème fraîche, a scattering of chopped chestnuts and a grating of nutmeg. Serve with the parmesan crisps.

Shallow-fried crispy balls of goat's cheese, with red onion marmalade and a rocket and fig salad, page 45

Light bites

V, GF, S, N
Trio of dips

We have been serving these in the restaurant for over five years now and they are still as popular as ever. They're great for a party or a lazy lunch; serve with warm flat bread cut into strips.

Serves 8

Roasted pepper and chilli hummus

2 x 400g tins of chick peas
2 cloves of garlic
half a red pepper, roasted, peeled and deseeded
half a yellow pepper, roasted, peeled and deseeded
2 tbsp lemon juice
2 tbsp water
1 tbsp olive oil
1 ½ tbsp tahini
1 tsp salt
1 tsp chilli powder
1 tbsp coriander leaves, finely chopped
1 tsp ground cumin

Place all the ingredients, except the coriander, in a blender – or use a hand blender in a bowl. Stir the coriander through the dip at the end.

Beetroot and mint dip

300g raw beetroot
1 clove of garlic
3 tbsp extra virgin olive oil
1½ tbsp tahini
2 tbsp red wine vinegar
1 tbsp chopped fresh mint leaves
salt and pepper

Preheat the oven to 180°C/gas mark 4. Sprinkle the beetroot with salt, wrap them in foil and put in a roasting tray. Bake them for 1–1½ hours, or until tender. Allow them to cool, peel off the skin and then blend the beetroot with the garlic, oil and tahini. Purée in a blender until the mixture is smooth. Transfer it to a bowl, stir in the vinegar and sprinkle with chopped mint. Season with salt and pepper.

Butternut tahini dip

500g butternut squash
salt and pepper
3 tbsp olive oil
½ tsp ground cinnamon
1 clove of garlic
1 tbsp tahini
1 tbsp lemon juice
2 tbsp pine nuts, toasted

Preheat the oven to 180°C/gas mark 4. Cut the butternut squash in half and place it in a roasting tray, cut side up. Season it with salt and pepper, drizzle it with 1 tablespoon of the olive oil and cover with foil. Roast it for 30 minutes, or until soft. Take it out of the oven and allow it to cool down a little.

Scoop the flesh out of the skin of the butternut squash and put it in a food processor or blender with the cinnamon, garlic, tahini, lemon juice and the remaining olive oil. Blend until smooth and season with salt and pepper. Sprinkle with the toasted pine nuts before serving.

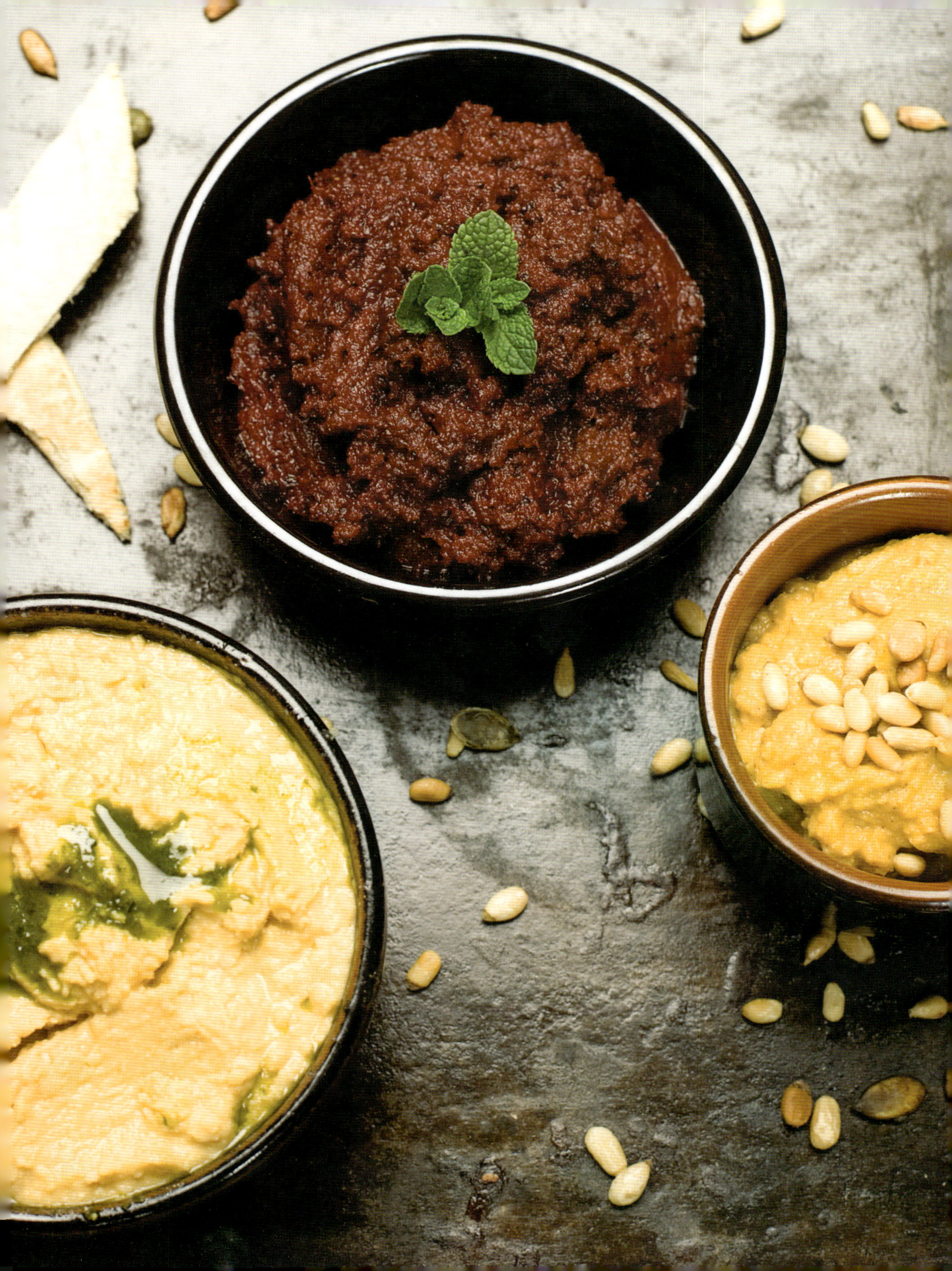

food for friends

Whole globe artichoke with three dips

GF

This would be a great dish for a dinner party starter to share or even on a buffet table for guests to pull off leaves and dip. Just make sure everyone knows only to eat the fleshy part of the leaves.

Serves 4

water
a slice of lemon
4 globe artichokes

For the tomato salsa:
3 medium plum tomatoes, chopped
half a medium onion, finely chopped
2 tbsp lemon juice
2 cloves of garlic, minced
3 tbsp fresh basil, chopped
¼ tsp salt
a small pinch of freshly ground black pepper

For the basil-infused oil:
300ml extra virgin olive oil
1 large bunch of basil

For the asparagus and 'parmesan' cream:
150ml double cream
4 tbsp grated vegetarian parmesan-style cheese
4 large spears of asparagus
15g butter
salt, pepper and paprika to taste

Fill a large bowl with water and put a slice of lemon in it. Cut the tough tips of the artichoke leaves off with scissors, holding the stalk to keep the artichoke steady. Using a knife, slice the base off so that it will sit upright. Pull the pale central leaves out, then scoop the feathery choke out with a spoon, without disturbing the heart underneath.

To prevent browning, drop each artichoke in the bowl of water as it is prepared. Put a large pan of salted water on a high heat, and add the artichokes when it boils. Reduce the heat slightly and cook the artichokes for 35–45 minutes (when they're ready you should be able to pull a leaf out easily).

While the artichokes are cooking, prepare the dips. Mix all the tomato salsa ingredients together and put them in a bowl. Set it aside until you are ready to serve.

To make the basil-infused oil, just blend the oil and basil together for about 4 minutes, and strain it through a fine sieve.

For the asparagus and parmesan cream, mix the cream and cheese together in a pan. Bring it almost to a boil, lower the heat and simmer for 5 minutes. Trim the ends of the asparagus, then blanch them for 1 minute in boiling salted water, and submerge them in iced water immediately. Put the asparagus into the cream sauce, add the butter and cook gently for 2 minutes, then blend into a smooth cream. Check the seasoning and add a little paprika.

When the artichokes are ready, remove them from the pan and drain them upside down. Allow them to cool slightly. Serve with the three dips; if you wish, you can remove the leaves and present them separately, or slice each one in half and present as shown opposite.

GFO
Ricotta, artichoke, spinach and 'parmesan' bakes

This is a lovely simple dish which we suggest as an appetiser or starter. It only takes ten minutes to make, tops, plus about ten to fifteen minutes in the oven. We like to serve it in little individual terracotta dishes, but you could make a bigger one to share or serve them in ramekins for a smaller portion. When we make these as a special in the restaurant we always run out! We have recommended corn tortillas as they are gluten free, however, you could make crostini by drizzling finely sliced bread with olive oil and lightly toasting.

Serves 8 as an appetiser

750g ricotta
2 cloves of garlic, peeled
50g fresh baby spinach
1 x 390g tin of artichoke hearts
fresh nutmeg, to grate
1 tsp salt
2 tbsp chopped fresh chives
1 tsp chopped fresh tarragon
100g fresh parmesan-style vegetarian cheese, grated – plus a little extra for sprinkling on top
corn tortilla chips, to serve

Preheat the oven to 180°C/gas mark 4. Using a food processor, blend the ricotta, garlic and spinach together until they form a smooth mixture. Add the artichoke hearts and a generous grating of fresh nutmeg (about a teaspoon), season with a sprinkling of salt and blend again. Stir in the chives, tarragon and parmesan. Spoon into the serving dishes, sprinkle the tops with parmesan and put in the oven for 10 minutes or until the tops are golden (if you are using a larger dish then this will take longer). Serve with a handful of tortilla chips to dunk into the bakes.

Shallow-fried crispy balls of goat's cheese, with red onion marmalade and a rocket and fig salad

The red onion marmalade can be made in advance, as can the balls of goat's cheese – just shape and coat them, then finish them just before you want to eat.

Serves 6

1 x 350g log of goat's cheese
1 medium bunch of basil, finely chopped
75g sun-dried tomatoes, finely chopped
a little dried polenta, for coating
500ml vegetable oil

For the red onion marmalade:
30g unsalted butter
250g red onions, finely sliced
3 tbsp red wine vinegar
75g caster sugar

For the rocket and fig salad:
1 packet of wild rocket leaves
6 vine tomatoes, sliced
a few shavings of parmesan-style vegetarian cheese
balsamic dressing (see page 8)
3 figs, halved
15g butter
2 tsp caster sugar

Make the red onion marmalade first. Melt the butter in a pan over a low to medium heat and gently sweat the onions for a good 10–12 minutes until they are really soft. Add the red wine vinegar and caster sugar, and stir frequently until there is almost no liquid left. Allow the mixture to cool and pour it into a sterilised glass jar with a lid (for ways of sterilising bottles, see page 10). It will keep in the fridge for up to 28 days, but once it has been opened use it within 7 days.

Then prepare the goat's cheese. Crumble the goat's cheese into a bowl and then mix in the basil and sun-dried tomato pieces. Form the mixture into little balls about 3cm in circumference, then roll them in the dried polenta.

When you are ready to serve, heat the vegetable oil in a large pan and fry the balls of goat's cheese for 3 minutes each.

Prepare the rocket and fig salad. Make a salad with the rocket leaves, tomatoes, vegetarian parmesan shavings and balsamic dressing. Take half a fig per person, heat the butter and sugar in a small frying pan, then place the cut side of the figs into the butter to caramelise for 2 minutes. Put them on top of the rocket salad and serve with the goat's cheese, accompanied by the red onion marmalade.

GF
Chargrilled asparagus with Béarnaise sauce and watercress and mature goat's cheese shavings

A Béarnaise sauce is an enriched version of a hollandaise sauce with a more pungent flavour, which comes from the tarragon and chervil. Before you start preparing the asparagus and sauce, make the watercress and hard goat's cheese salad and put it onto the plates with the dressing. Both the asparagus and the sauce will be ready very quickly and should be eaten straight away.

Serves 4

a large bunch of fresh asparagus (ideally 3–4 spears per person)
a little vegetable oil
salt and pepper

For the salad:
250g watercress
a handful of hard goat's cheese shavings
balsamic dressing (see page 8)

For the Béarnaise sauce:
1 shallot, peeled and finely chopped
4 tsp chopped tarragon
2 tsp chopped chervil
75ml dry white wine
75ml white wine vinegar
pinch of crushed white peppercorns
pinch of salt
225g unsalted butter
3 egg yolks, at room temperature
freshly ground pepper

Make the salad with the watercress and hard goat's cheese shavings, and dress it with some balsamic dressing. Set it to one side.

Bring a pan of water to the boil and add a teaspoon of salt. Bend one of the asparagus spears until it snaps, then cut the rest of the bunch to the same length. When the water has boiled, drop the spears in, cut end first, and cook for 3 minutes. Put a bowl of iced water close by. Drain the asparagus spears and plunge them into the water, then take them out immediately. Put them on a chopping board or large plate, drizzle with a little vegetable oil and season with salt and pepper.

To make the sauce put the shallot, 1 tsp of the tarragon, ½ tsp of the chervil, the white wine and the vinegar into a saucepan. Add the peppercorns and salt and bring to a boil, cooking until the liquid has reduced by two thirds. Strain through a fine strainer or a muslin-lined sieve and allow to cool. The liquid will be about 3 tbsp at this point. Melt the butter in a pan over a low heat until it starts to foam. Cook for one minute until the foam turns whitish. Skim off the foam and discard. Allow the butter to cool enough so that you can dip your little finger in. In a blender whizz together the egg yolks and reduction, or use a hand blender. Slowly add the butter in a thin and steady stream, continuously whisking until a light sauce is formed. Stir in the remaining tarragon and chervil and check seasoning. Keep warm until needed.

Put a lightly oiled griddle over a high heat. When the griddle pan is hot, chargrill the asparagus for a minute on either side. Serve it immediately with the sauce, accompanied by the salad.

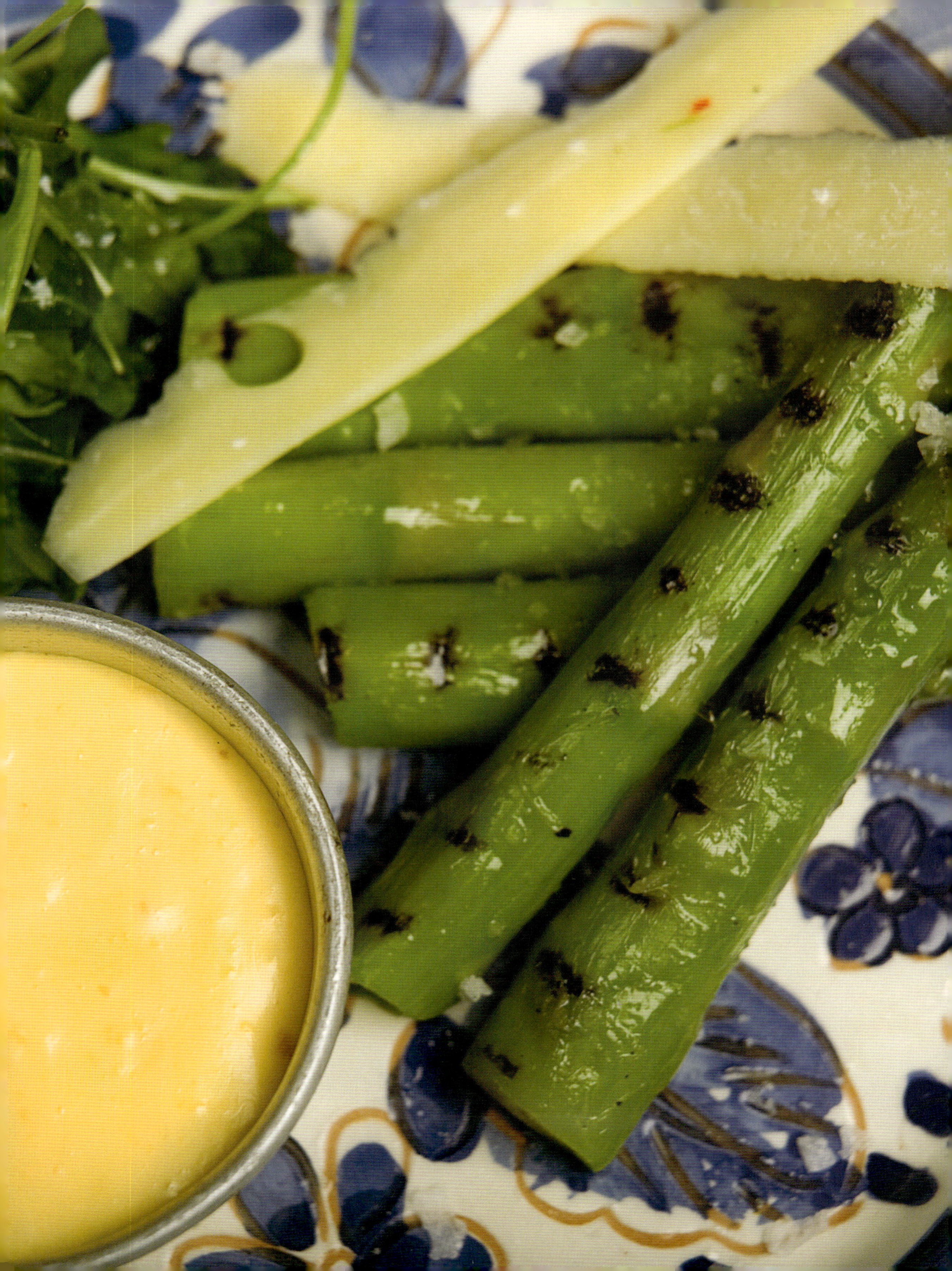

Persian cauliflower kuku

In the Middle East, eggs are very popular and form a staple part of the diet. Many people start their day with a breakfast of fried eggs, fresh bread, walnuts and a type of cheese similar to a mild feta. Iranians are especially fond of an egg dish called kuku, a type of omelette similar to an Italian frittata and the Arabic eggah. Kuku is filled with vegetables or herbs and is delicious eaten straight from the oven or fridge. It can be served as an appetiser with bread, or as a simple lunch or supper with yoghurt, salad and bread. Kuku is also ideal for picnics; just serve it in some crusty bread.

This is a take on a favourite kuku which is made with cauliflower and is a little more elaborate than most, but you could use any vegetable – such as courgettes, aubergines, asparagus, mushrooms or spinach – instead.

Serves 6

6 eggs
½ tsp baking powder
1 tbsp flour
120ml milk or soya milk
120g parmesan-style vegetarian cheese, grated
4 tbsp vegetable oil or 60g butter
1 small red onion, peeled and thinly sliced
2 cloves of garlic, peeled and crushed
1 small head of cauliflower, coarsely chopped into pieces approximately 2cm square
2 tsp salt
½ tsp freshly ground black pepper
1 tsp ground cumin
¼ tsp ground paprika
¼ tsp turmeric
a pinch of cayenne pepper
4 tbsp chopped parsley

Whisk the eggs in a mixing bowl and then add the baking powder, flour, milk and cheese. Whisk everything together lightly.

Using a medium-sized non-stick frying pan, heat the oil or butter over a low heat. Add the onion and cook it until translucent for about 5 minutes; do not let it brown. Add the garlic, cauliflower, salt, pepper, cumin, paprika, turmeric and parsley and stir-fry them for about 10 minutes or until the cauliflower is soft.

Pour the egg mixture over the cauliflower in the pan and cook it over a low heat for about 10 minutes until it has set. Turn the grill to a medium temperature and place the pan underneath to brown the top of the kuku. Turn it out onto a plate and either serve it hot or put it aside to cool down.

V, N

Chestnut mushroom, chervil and pine nut paté with a pear and plum chutney

This is another versatile dish that could be used as a starter at Christmas or part of a summer buffet. Our favourite is to make miniature melba toasts with a teaspoon of paté and a tiny bit of chutney on top. If you are not vegan you can use butter instead of margarine and single cream instead of the soya cream.

Serves 6–8

350g chestnut mushrooms, sliced
3 cloves garlic, finely chopped
150g vegan margarine
1 tsp grated nutmeg
zest and juice of 1 lemon
70g pine nuts, toasted
1 medium bunch of chervil, chopped
1½ tbsp Dijon mustard
1 x 200ml carton of soya cream
300g fresh breadcrumbs
salt and pepper
a little oil
melba toasts and pear and plum chutney, to serve

Warm a large frying pan over a medium heat and sauté the mushrooms and garlic in the vegan margarine until they are soft; stir in the nutmeg towards the end of the cooking time. Take the pan off the heat. Add the lemon juice and zest, pine nuts, chervil, mustard and soya cream. Stir to combine, then add the breadcrumbs. Season with salt and pepper and mix everything together well.

Pour a very little oil into a 900g (2lb) bread tin and swirl it around, then line the tin with cling film – the oil will help the cling film to stick to the sides. Pack the paté mixture into the tin, cover it with more cling film and any film that overlaps the edges of the tin, and leave it in the fridge to set overnight, or for at least 4 hours. Serve with melba toast and pear and plum chutney (see page 14).

Sweet potato, garlic and rosemary gratin with a red pepper sauce, page 62

Pastas and bakes

VO, GFO
Pappardelle with rocket and pine nut pesto, with griddled Mediterranean vegetables and parmesan

This is a simple supper recipe that is really quick to make. For a vegan option leave out the cheese; if you need a gluten-free option, use gluten-free pasta. Ideally the best way to cook the vegetables is on a griddle pan; however you could either use a large hot frying pan or even just roast the vegetables in the oven.

Serves 4 hungry people, or 6 as a light lunch

- 2 red peppers, tops and middles removed
- 2 yellow peppers, tops and middles removed
- 3 courgettes, cut into 5mm strips lengthways
- 2 aubergines, cut into 5mm strips lengthways
- a little olive oil
- half a medium bunch of thyme, leaves only, finely chopped
- 1 quantity basil, rocket and pine nut pesto (see page 7)
- 1 tsp salt
- 500g pappardelle (ideally fresh)
- 100g parmesan-style vegetarian cheese shavings
- black pepper

Brush all the vegetables with olive oil. Heat a griddle pan until it is hot and griddle the vegetables separately, as each one will take a different time; for example, the aubergines will take approximately 10 minutes on each side, the peppers and courgettes should take 5 minutes on each side. Set them to one side as they are cooked, allowing them to cool down. When the vegetables have all been cooked, and are all cool, chop them into pretty triangles and then put them in a bowl and add the thyme; mix them together. Set to one side.

Put the pesto in a bowl. Bring a large pan of water to the boil and add a teaspoon of salt. When it comes to the boil cook the pappardelle for 5 minutes. Drain well, and then mix the pasta into the pesto and stir in the vegetables. Using a vegetable peeler, peel fine ribbons from a piece of parmesan to top the pasta (you can scatter some grated parmesan over it if you prefer). Season with black pepper and serve.

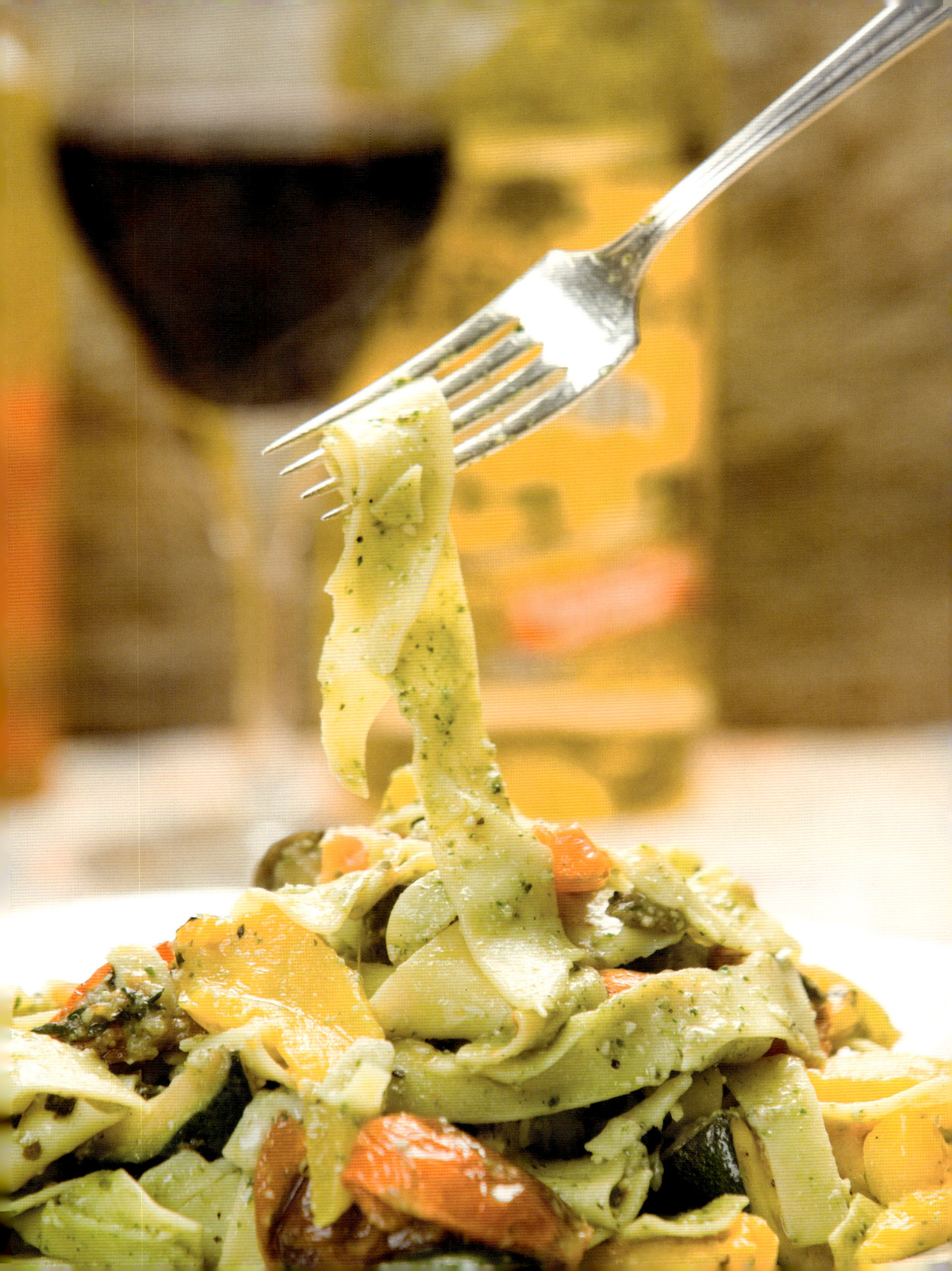

GO
Spinach and ricotta gnocchi carbonara with smoked garlic

This is a great supper or easy lunch recipe that children seem to enjoy as well – and our children don't seem to notice the spinach, either! This recipe is also very easy to make into a gluten-free dish; replace the semolina with gluten-free flour and roll the gnocchi in that too, instead of the plain flour. You can also substitute any good vegetarian Italian or English hard cheese for the parmesan.

Serves 4

3 cloves smoked garlic
150g baby spinach leaves
170g ricotta
60g coarsely ground semolina
60g parmesan-style vegetarian cheese, finely grated
1 egg, beaten
a little freshly grated nutmeg
salt and black pepper
2 tbsp plain flour, for shaping the gnocchi
a few parmesan shavings

For the carbonara sauce:
1 tbsp butter
1 small onion, finely chopped
4 egg yolks
6 tablespoons single cream
60g grated parmesan-style vegetarian cheese
2 tbsp fresh parsley, finely chopped

Preheat the oven to 160°C/gas mark 3.

Finely slice the garlic cloves and place in a baking tray. Roast in the oven for 4 minutes before taking out and leaving to cool. Blanch the baby spinach in boiling water for 30 seconds and squeeze, removing all the water. Chop up the spinach.

Put the spinach, ricotta, semolina, parmesan and beaten egg in a food processor and blend them well. Then season the mixture with the nutmeg, salt and pepper. Dust a tray or work surface with plain flour and spoon the gnocchi dough onto it. Form it into a long sausage and roll it over until evenly coated. Then cut the roll into gnocchi pieces 2cm thick.

Bring a large pan of salted water to the simmer and gently poach the gnocchi, a few at a time, for about 2–3 minutes until they rise to the surface; do not allow the water to boil. Remove the gnocchi with a slotted spoon when they surface and allow them to drain before setting them to one side; keep going until all the gnocchi have been poached. Keep them warm in a low oven while you make the sauce.

Heat the butter in a small pan and gently fry the onion until soft and golden. Whisk the carbonara sauce ingredients together in a bowl add to pan. Stir over a very low heat until the sauce thickens – approximately 3–4 minutes.

Carefully put the gnocchi on the serving plates and spoon the sauce over them; top with the shaved cheese and sprinkle the smoked garlic over the top. Serve, accompanied by garlic bread and a crisp salad with tomatoes.

VO, GFO
Penne with spinach, portobello mushrooms and green beans with a sundried tomato, black olive and truffle-oil tapenade

Here is another simple pasta recipe. We have suggested penne but feel free to experiment with your own favourite fresh pasta.

Serves 8

a pinch of salt
800g small penne, ideally fresh, gluten-free if necessary
200g fine green beans, chopped
250g sun-dried tomatoes
250g pitted black olives
3 tbsp sunflower oil
4 cloves of garlic, peeled
3 tbsp white truffle oil
2 tbsp vegan margarine or butter
3 shallots, peeled and finely sliced
4 large portobello mushrooms, halved and then finely sliced
150g fresh baby spinach
100g parmesan-style vegetarian cheese (optional)

Bring a large pan of cold water to boil with the salt. Cook the pasta according to the packet instructions. Drain it through a colander but keep half of the pasta water. Refresh the pasta with cold water and set it aside. While the pasta is cooking, lightly steam the green beans and set them to one side.

Using a food processor, blend the sun-dried tomatoes into a paste, then add the olives, sunflower oil, garlic and truffle oil and blend this tapenade mixture again.

Melt the margarine or butter and sauté the shallots in a large pan. When they are soft, add the mushrooms and sauté until they are golden brown and also soft. Then stir the tapenade into the pan and allow it to cook for a few minutes.

Add a ladle of the pasta water to the pan and then add the pasta, stirring it through so that it is coated in the tapenade. Add the baby spinach leaves to the pan and allow them to wilt a little. Then add the cooked green beans and stir through. If the dish looks too dry, add a little more of the pasta water and stir thoroughly.

Pour the pasta into a warm serving dish, sprinkle with freshly grated parmesan, if desired, and serve with hot crusty garlic bread.

GF
Puy lentil, aubergine and red wine moussaka

This moussaka looks really nice when served in individual terracotta dishes: especially effective if you are trying to impress. It's equally good made in larger baking dishes, and it's great for supper or lunch with friends when served with a big bowl of salad.

Serves 8 hungry people

2 large onions, peeled and diced
150ml olive oil or vegetable oil
3 tsp ground cumin
3 tsp ground allspice
500g Puy lentils
4 cloves of garlic, finely chopped
250ml full-bodied red wine
200g of ripe, fresh tomatoes, chopped, or 175g tinned chopped tomatoes
1 tbsp vegetable oil
4–5 large aubergines, topped and tailed, sliced into 1cm rounds

For the moussaka topping:
750g full-fat Greek yoghurt
2 eggs, beaten
1½ tsp sugar
1 tsp salt
a little freshly grated nutmeg
1 goats' cheese log and black olives (optional)

Preheat the oven to 180°C/gas mark 4. Using a large saucepan over a medium heat, sweat the onions in the oil until they are soft but not coloured. Add the spices, lentils and garlic, and stir thoroughly making sure the lentils are coated in the oil. When you smell the aroma of the spices from the pan, and they are thoroughly mixed with the lentils, add the wine and tomatoes. Put a lid on the pan and cook for approximately 45 minutes to an hour until the lentils are cooked through (Puy lentils are supposed to have a bit of bite). It's a good idea to give them a quick stir every 10 minutes so they don't stick to the bottom of the pan. If for some reason they do and it smells burnt, then take the pan off the heat immediately. Transfer the lentils to a clean pan, without scraping the bottom of the old one – otherwise you will have a smoke-flavoured moussaka, which is not nice.

Cover the bottom of a baking tray with some vegetable oil and then lie the aubergine slices in the tray, turning them over once in the oil so they are coated on both sides. Roast them in the oven for 10–15 minutes until they are quite soft and have started to colour. They don't need to be completely cooked; this is just a pre-roast before they go in the moussaka.

Make the moussaka topping by mixing the yoghurt, eggs, salt, sugar and nutmeg in a bowl, and set it to one side. Grease whatever baking dishes you are going to use.

Put a layer of aubergines in the bottom of the baking dish. Then generously ladle a layer of the lentil stew over them followed by a layer of aubergines, and so on. Make sure you leave enough space for the yoghurt sauce at the top as it should be nice and thick so that the aubergines beneath it don't dry out (this is particularly important if you are using small dishes; leave at least 1cm). Use a palette knife to make it nice and smooth.

Decorate the top, if you wish, with slices of goats' cheese log and black olives. Put the moussaka in the oven and cook until it is smelling delicious and the top is nicely browned – this will take about 45 minutes for a large dish, and around 30 minutes for individual ones.

We serve this with a tomato, red onion and baby leaf salad with a lemon and olive oil dressing, but any sharply dressed salad would do.

GFO, N
Oven-baked beetroot gnocchi with melted cherry vine tomatoes, roasted fennel and pesto

Serves 6

3kg Maris Piper or other firm white potatoes, skins on
4 whole fennel bulbs
olive oil, as necessary
salt and pepper
18 small cherry tomatoes
3 beetroot, steamed or boiled until soft, and peeled
450g plain flour or 400g gluten-free flour
4 eggs, beaten
200g parmesan-style vegetarian cheese, grated
a little vegetable oil
1 tsp butter
1 clove of garlic, crushed
150ml basil, rocket and pine nut pesto (see page 7)
a handful of toasted pine nuts, to garnish
freshly grated parmesan-style vegetarian cheese, to garnish

Preheat the oven to 180°C/gas mark 4. Put the potatoes in a large pan of cold salted water, bring it to the boil and cook for 45 minutes or until the potatoes are soft all the way through. When the potatoes are ready, drain the water off and refill the pan with cold water to help cool them down.

Top and tail the fennel bulbs and then cut out the hard core in the middle. Cut into chunks about 2cm wide by 6cm long. Drizzle generously with olive oil and season with salt and pepper. Place on a baking tray, cover tightly with foil and cook in the preheated oven for 10 minutes.

Wash and dry the cherry tomatoes and put them on another baking tray. Drizzle with a little olive oil, season with salt and pepper and roast them in the oven too, also for 10 minutes or until they are soft. Take the tomatoes and fennel out of the oven and keep them warm under foil. Turn the oven up to 200°C/gas mark 6.

When the potatoes are cool, peel the skins off. Mash them together with the cooked beetroot using a potato masher and then a fork or, ideally, by using a potato ricer. Mix them thoroughly with a wooden spoon to make an evenly pink mash. Add the flour, eggs and grated parmesan, and season with salt to taste. Mix thoroughly with a clean hand and, if necessary, add a tablespoon of vegetable oil to make the mixture come together.

Take a handful of the mixture and roll it into a long sausage. Then cut it into chunky nuggets and do so until all of the mixture is used up. Drizzle a little vegetable oil in baking tray and put the gnocchi on it. Cook them in the oven for 7–8 minutes so they have a slightly golden colour.

In a frying pan, melt the butter and add the crushed garlic clove. Just as it starts to brown, add a little salt and pepper and remove the pan from the heat. Add the basil pesto and stir it around, then add the gnocchi to the pan and toss them in the warmed pesto.

Serve with the warm roasted tomatoes and the roasted fennel – and a scattering of toasted pine nuts and fresh parmesan if you wish.

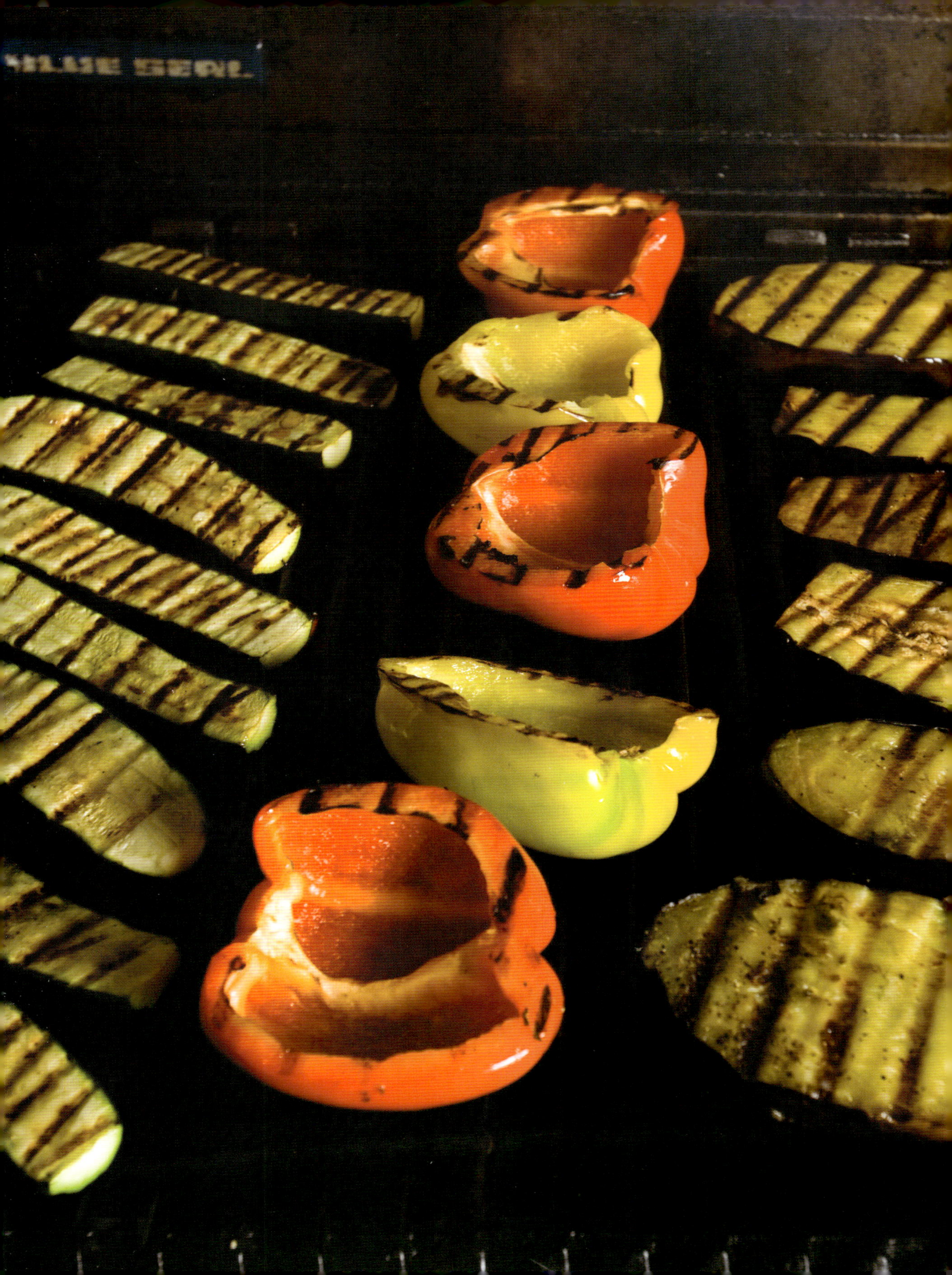

Roasted Mediterranean vegetable lasagne topped with a goat's cheese, chive and walnut sauce

The precise amount of lasagne you need for this dish will depend on how many layers you can fit in the ovenproof dish you will be using. It should be quite large – about 35cm x 25cm. In the restaurant we serve this lasagne with home-made garlic bread and a crispy leaf salad.

Serves 6

250g butter
1 large onion, finely chopped
4 cloves of garlic, chopped
400g soft goat's cheese, roughly chopped
500ml double cream
1 small bunch of chives, finely chopped
salt and pepper
20g shelled walnuts, crumbled into small pieces
3 red peppers, deseeded and sliced into 1cm strips
3 yellow peppers, deseeded and sliced into 1cm strips
a little olive oil
200g plain flour
600ml milk
2 large aubergines, topped and tailed, cut into thin slices lengthways
300g dried lasagne sheets
500g courgettes, cut in slices lengthways

Preheat the oven to 180°C/gas mark 4. Using a large shallow pan, melt half the butter and add the finely chopped onion. Sweat the onions for 5 minutes, then add the garlic and cook for another 10 minutes. Add the goat's cheese and cream, and stir with a wooden spoon for 10 minutes, then add the chives. Season with salt and pepper and add the walnuts. Continue to stir until the sauce thickens, then set it aside. Place the peppers in a baking tray, drizzle them with a little olive oil, season with salt and pepper and roast in the oven for 10 minutes or until soft.

To make the béchamel sauce for the lasagne, melt the remaining butter in a saucepan, add the flour and stir it through to allow the flour to cook. When it starts to lift away from the pan like a soft dough add the milk bit by bit, stirring all the time to create a smooth white sauce. Assemble the lasagne. Grease the dish with a little oil and then place a layer of aubergine slices on the bottom, ladle on some of the goat's cheese sauce, then add a layer of lasagne sheets, followed by a layer of roasted peppers, more sauce, then a layer of courgettes – and repeat this process again until there is a small space at the top.

Pour the béchamel sauce over the lasagne, and put it in the oven for 45 minutes until golden brown on top and cooked through.

V, GF
Sweet potato, garlic and rosemary gratin with red pepper sauce

This is one of the all-time favourites in the restaurant. The dish is not only delicious but meets various dietary requirements. We serve it with dressed rocket and seasonal griddled vegetables. Alternatively you could serve the gratin with some pan-fried mushrooms instead of the roasted mediterranean vegetables.

Serves 6

4 cloves of garlic, chopped
1 tsp salt
1 tsp black pepper
150ml olive oil
1 large sweet potato
3 large white or red potatoes
3 tbsp of rosemary, finely chopped
1 tbsp of thyme leaves, finely chopped
a quarter quantity of red pepper sauce
   (approx 75ml, see page 3)

Preheat the oven to 180°C/gas mark 4. Blend the garlic, salt, pepper, and oil together in a blender (or use a hand blender). Place the resulting mixture in a large container. Finely slice the sweet potato and the ordinary potatoes, and put the slices into the container. Add the chopped rosemary and thyme and allow the potatoes to infuse with the oil and garlic mix for 10 minutes.

Line a 2cm deep baking tray, approximately 25cm by 15cm, with baking paper. Put the potato mix in the tray, pressing it down into the corners to make sure the there is an even amount across the tray. Cover the surface with another piece of baking paper and cook in the oven for 35 minutes. Take it out of the oven. Get another tray the same size and press down on top of the gratin to squeeze out the excess juices; tip the trays to allow them to drain. Then put the gratin back in the oven for another 20 minutes or so, until golden in colour. Check the middle with a knife to see if it is cooked.

Turn the gratin upside-down over a chopping board and lift the tray off. Then carefully remove the paper and trim the edges. Drizzle the red pepper sauce around the gratin when you serve it.

For a simple meal, accompany this with a handful of dressed rocket leaves. If you are trying to impress, then serve the gratin on a bed of roasted Mediterranean vegetables, but still accompanied by a rocket salad and the red pepper sauce. Just take a courgette, an aubergine and a couple of peppers, chop them into big chunks, toss in olive oil, or an oil flavoured with herbs or garlic and salt and pepper and roast in a 200°C/gas mark 6 oven for 15 minutes.

Butternut squash, sweet potato and dolcelatte lasagne

This is a very comforting dish ideal for those cold winter days and nights. Some blue cheeses are not vegetarian – always check the label for animal rennet.

Serves 6–8

200g butter
2 cloves of garlic, chopped
1 medium onion, chopped
570ml double cream
1 tsp salt
150g dolcelatte, or other vegetarian blue cheese, crumbled
1 tbsp finely chopped thyme leaves
3 tbsp finely chopped parsley, including stalks
250g plain flour
550ml milk
fresh nutmeg, for grating
250g butternut squash, peeled
250g sweet potato, peeled
1 x 250g box of lasagne sheets
a little grated parmesan-style vegetarian cheese (optional)
2–3 tomatoes, sliced (optional)

Preheat the oven to 180°C/gas mark 4 and grease a large ovenproof dish (or two medium ones).

Melt 75g of the butter in a saucepan over a medium heat, and then add the onion, followed by the garlic. Cook until they are soft and golden in colour. Add the cream and salt and stir until the cream starts to thicken; do not let it boil. Just before boiling point is reached, add the dolcelatte and stir until it has melted completely. Then stir in the thyme and parsley and take the pan off the heat.

Make the béchamel sauce for the lasagne. Melt the remaining butter in a saucepan, add the flour and stir through to allow the flour to cook. Keep stirring until the flour starts to pull away from the bottom of the pan. Gradually add the milk, and whisk everything together. Keep whisking until the sauce starts to thicken, which will take 5–8 minutes. Grate a generous amount of nutmeg and stir it through.

Using a food processor or sharp knife, cut the butternut squash and sweet potatoes into fine slices about 3mm thick. Take the prepared dish and put a layer of sweet potato slices over the bottom lengthways, making sure you cover the surface of the dish. Ladle the cheese sauce over the sweet potato and be generous, as this layer will help to steam and cook the pasta sheets.

Place one layer of lasagne sheets on top of the cheese sauce. Then put a layer of butternut squash horizontally across the dish. Follow that with a layer of cheese sauce, followed by lasagne and so on. When the layering is complete, generously ladle the thick béchamel sauce over the top. Sprinkle with a little grated parmesan if you wish; you can also decorate the top with some sliced tomatoes.

Bake the lasagne in the oven for 40–45 minutes, by which time it should have a golden top. Serve it with some steamed green beans or a green salad and garlic bread.

VO, N
Aubergine, pomegranate and walnut bake

This is a version of a Persian dish from the Caspian region of Iran. It really is very delicious and can be served with either steamed basmati rice or couscous. You should be able to find bottles of pomegranate molasses in large supermarkets' ethnic sections, but you can also order it online – there isn't really a substitute.

Serves 4

- 2 large aubergines, peeled
- 120ml olive oil
- 4 cloves of garlic
- 225g toasted walnuts
- 120ml pomegranate molasses
- 1 tbsp honey (for vegan option use maple syrup)
- 2 tsp ground cumin
- ¼ tsp ground cinnamon
- 1 tsp salt
- ¼ tsp black pepper
- ¼ tsp turmeric
- 1 small red chilli, deseeded and chopped finely
- 4 tbsp fresh parsley, finely chopped
- 75g spring onions, finely chopped
- 4 tbsp fresh coriander, finely chopped
- pomegranate seeds, for garnish

Preheat the oven to 200°C/gas mark 6. Slice the aubergines into slices about 5mm thick by 7cm long, and put them in a colander with a sprinkling of salt for 15 minutes to remove any bitterness. Then rinse them with water and dry them off. Put the slices on an oiled baking sheet and brush one side with the olive oil, then turn them over and brush the other side. Roast them in the oven for 15 minutes until they have a golden colour.

Using a food processor, mix the garlic, walnuts, pomegranate molasses, honey, cumin, cinnamon, salt and pepper, turmeric, chilli, parsley, spring onions and coriander until you have a grainy paste. Adjust the seasoning to your liking; if it's too sweet add more pomegranate molasses, or add some more honey if it isn't sweet enough.

Arrange a layer of aubergines in an oven-proof dish about 2cm deep and then alternate with the walnut sauce until you have used all the aubergine. Cover the dish with a lid or tightly wrapped foil, put it in the oven and cook for 50 minutes.

Remove the dish from the oven. Garnish the bake with pomegranate seeds and serve with steamed basmati rice (follow recipe on page 73 to the end of the second paragraph).

Paprika-flavoured oyster and enocchi mushrooms with smoked tofu, pan-fried polenta and carrot and mint purée, page 70

Noodles, grains and pulses

V, GF, N

Flash in the pan stir-fried vegetables with tofu, cashew and peanuts, served on nori with a choice of spicy teriyaki or amae sauce

This dish, broadly speaking, follows the guidelines for a macrobiotic diet as it uses ingredients such as high-fibre brown rice, soy products such as tofu and tamari, and fresh land and sea vegetables. We serve the stir-fry on nori sheets with organic brown rice. However, if you prefer you can serve it with healthy noodles such as those made from buckwheat. We have recommended two sauces here – the amae is sweeter and the teriyaki is more spicy.

Serves 6

1 white or red onion, finely chopped
1 sweet potato, peeled and cut into fine strips
150g mangetout, cut into strips
2 large carrots, peeled and cut into fine strips
1 red pepper, deseeded and cut into fine strips
1 yellow pepper, deseeded and cut into fine strips
2 courgettes, sliced or diced
250g oyster mushrooms, chopped
1 bunch of spring onions, topped and tailed, sliced into 2cm pieces
a large handful of coriander leaves, chopped
2 tbsp vegetable oil
100g cashew nuts, toasted
150g firm tofu, chopped into 1cm cubes and fried in a little oil
100g unsalted peanuts, toasted
6 sheets of nori seaweed

For the spicy teriyaki sauce:
15g ginger, sliced but not peeled
4 tbsp sweet chilli sauce
3 tbsp tamari
1 small red chilli, deseeded and finely chopped
1 tbsp brown sugar
100ml water
2 cinnamon sticks
4 star anise

For the amae sauce:
3 tbsp malt vinegar
3 tbsp caster sugar
6 tbsp tamari
1½ tbsp tomato ketchup
2 tsp tamarind paste
1 tsp brown sugar

Prepare your choice of sauce first. For the teriyaki sauce, put the ginger, sweet chilli sauce, tamari, fresh chilli, brown sugar and water in a small saucepan. Stir them together and put over a medium heat. As it heats up, drop the cinnamon sticks and the star anise into the saucepan. Simmer it for 20 minutes, then drain it through a sieve into a bowl. You should end up with about 200ml of sauce.

Or you may prefer the amae sauce. In a small saucepan gently heat the vinegar and dissolve the sugar into it. Then add the rest of the amae sauce ingredients, stirring thoroughly. Take it off the heat.

In a large bowl, mix all the stir-fry vegetables using your hands. Heat the oil in a large wok to a high temperature – it will start to glisten. Carefully put all the vegetables in and then add the cashews and tofu cubes, constantly stirring and moving the pan to stop the ingredients sticking. Cook until slightly softened, which should be about 10 minutes depending on how al dente you like vegetables. After about 8 minutes of cooking pour in the sauce you have chosen and stir it through thoroughly.

Take the toasted peanuts and blitz them with a hand blender. Serve the stir-fry with wholegrain high-fibre buckwheat noodles or organic brown basmati rice, and sprinkle the peanuts on top.

V
Paprika-flavoured oyster and enocchi mushrooms with smoked tofu, pan-fried polenta and carrot and mint purée

Serves 6

3 tbsp olive oil
1 onion, peeled and finely chopped
5 cloves of garlic, finely chopped
1 red pepper, deseeded and diced
1 yellow pepper, deseeded and diced
1 large bunch of thyme
½ red chilli, finely sliced
2 litres vegetable stock
salt and pepper
500g polenta (fine)
250g smoked tofu, drained and cut into cubes
500g oyster mushrooms
2 punnets of enocchi mushrooms (found in Oriental or Asian supermarkets)
50g vegan margarine
125g shallots, peeled and chopped
2 tsp smoked paprika
1 large bag of baby spinach leaves

For the carrot and mint puree:
10 small carrots
150g vegan margarine
1 bunch of fresh mint
salt and pepper

Lightly grease and line a baking tray or ceramic dish (approximately 20cm by 30cm) with baking paper. You will also need a 7cm diameter ring or something similar for cutting the polenta.

Heat the olive oil in a large saucepan and gently sweat the onion for 5 minutes. Then add the garlic, peppers, thyme and chilli and cook for a further 3 minutes. Add the stock and bring to the boil. Season generously with salt and pepper and then gradually add the polenta a little at a time, whisking continuously to stop the polenta becoming lumpy. Lower the heat a little to allow the polenta to cook and stir it with a wooden spoon. Then pour the polenta mix into the lined baking tray and smooth it over with the back of a knife, spreading it out evenly. Put it to one side for 1 hour, allowing it to cool and set.

To make the carrot and mint puree, top and tail the carrots and then chop them into three pieces each. Place in a pan of cold water, bring to the boil and cook for 20–25 minutes until they are cooked and soft enough to mash. Drain them, add the margarine and then mash until smooth. Add the chopped mint and season with salt and pepper. Keep the purée warm while you prepare the mushrooms.

To prepare the oyster mushrooms, tear them into long strips by hand. Cut off the roots of the enocchi mushrooms and again separate them by hand.

Melt the margarine in a frying pan. Add the shallots and tofu and fry for 2 minutes on a medium heat, stirring all the while. Add the oyster mushrooms and cook for 6 minutes on a high heat. Finally add the enocchi and paprika, season with salt and pepper and cook for a further 2 minutes so that all of the mushrooms are soft and smelling delicious.

When you are ready to eat, take a cutter and cut out six pieces of the cold polenta. Pan fry these in a little oil for 2 minutes on each side. Then pan-fry the baby spinach with a little margarine. Serve the polenta on top of the spinach with the smoked tofu and mushrooms placed on top of the discs of polenta, and with the carrot and mint purée on the side.

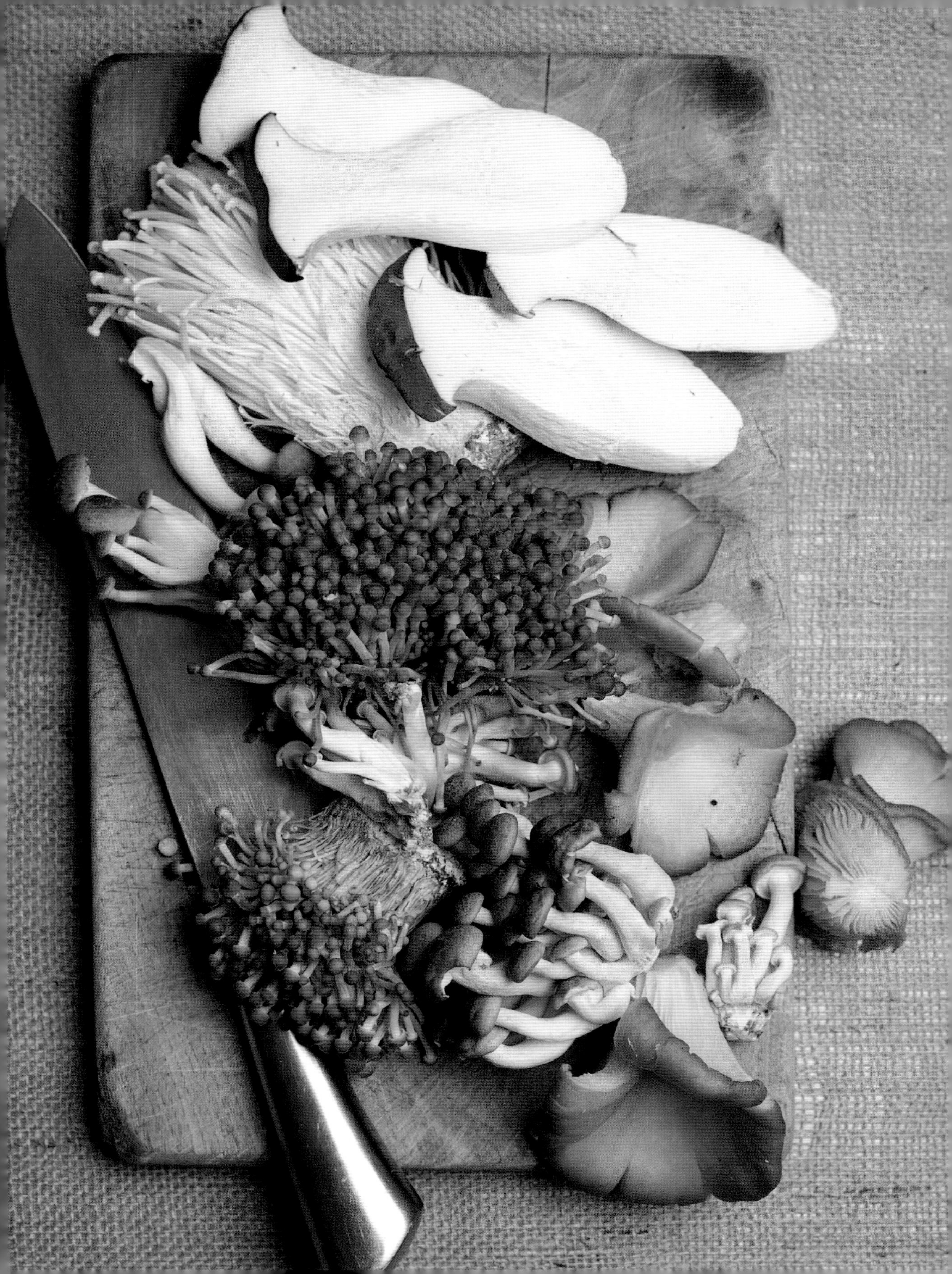

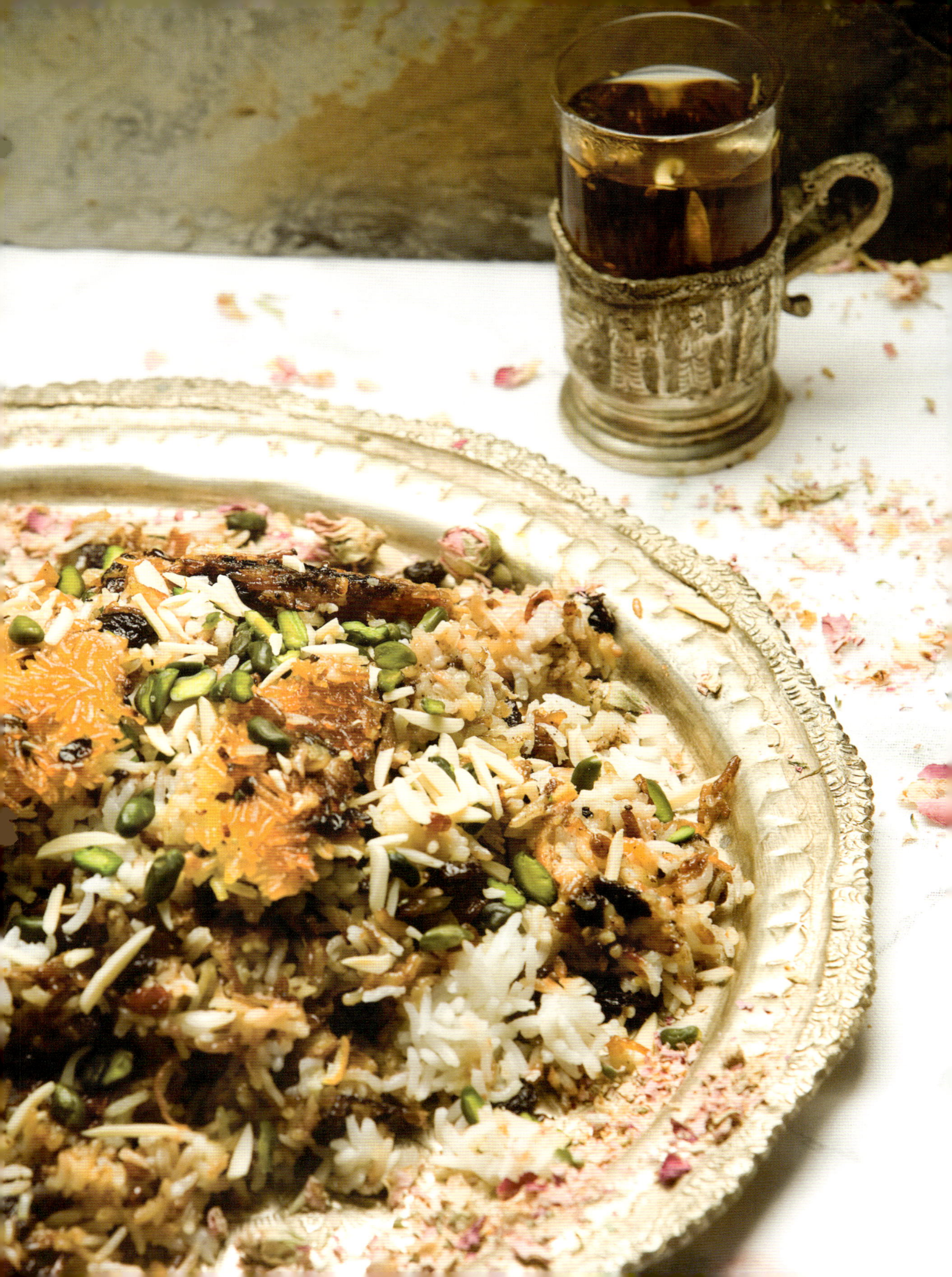

VO, GF, N
Persian rice with sour cherries, chickpeas, pistachios and almonds

In Iran, people tend to eat khoreshes, which are slow-cooked casseroles made from meat or vegetables with herbs and served with rice, or they eat polows which are when herbs, vegetables or meat are added and cooked in layers through the rice. This recipe is a delicious polow which should also give you a tadik, the crispy rice at the bottom which people always seem to associate with Iranian food. You can find the sour cherries in ethnic supermarkets or health-food shops.

Serves 4

300g long-grain white basmati rice
600ml water, (for cooking rice)
4 tbsp vegetable oil
2 tsp salt
1 medium onion, peeled and thinly sliced
2.5cm piece of fresh ginger, peeled and grated
1 cinnamon stick 5cm long, or 1 tsp ground cinnamon
1 x 400g tin of chickpeas, drained and rinsed
150g pitted dried sour cherries
½ tsp cayenne
½ tsp ground saffron threads, dissolved in 2 tbsp hot water
3 tbsp caster sugar
3 tbsp pomegranate molasses
100ml water
75g shelled unsalted pistachios (slivered)
75g blanched toasted almonds (slivered)

Prepare the rice by putting it in a large bowl and covering it with lukewarm water. Agitate it gently by hand and then pour off the water. Repeat this 4 to 5 times until the rice is completely clean and there is no starch in the water.

Use a medium-sized non-stick saucepan. Put the rice in and add the 600ml water, 2 tablespoons of the oil and the salt, and bring it to the boil. When the water has been absorbed reduce the heat to medium, and cover the pan with a tea towel wrapped around the lid. Do not touch the rice; just allow it to cook for 20 minutes.

Heat the remaining oil in a deep frying pan over a high-to-medium heat. When it is very hot, add the onion, ginger and cinnamon and fry them for 10 minutes, stirring all the time until the onions are golden brown. Add the chickpeas, dried cherries, cayenne, saffron and sugar, pomegranate molasses and 100ml water. Bring to the boil, add the slivered pistachios and almonds and stir them through. Then remove the pan from the heat. Add this cherry mix to the rice and fluff it through with a fork. Cover the pan firmly again to prevent the steam escaping, and cook it on the lowest possible heat for another 15 minutes.

Transfer the rice to a serving dish. Carefully remove the crusty rice at the bottom of the pan and decorate the top of the rice with it; serve with a green salad.

VO, GF
Pinto bean chilli

Serve this with steamed basmati rice or our favourite – taco shells, sour cream, guacamole and grated cheddar cheese. For a vegan option omit the sour cream and cheddar cheese and use a tomato salsa.

Serves 6–8

400g dried pinto beans
2 tbsp vegetable oil
1 large onion, finely diced
2 stalks of celery, finely chopped
1 small red chilli (deseeded or not, depending on your taste)
6 cloves of garlic, chopped
450g ripe, fresh, chopped tomatoes
450ml fresh vegetable stock

For the spice mix:
1 tsp cayenne pepper
2 tsp ground coriander
3 tsp ground cumin
2 tsp dried mixed herbs

Soak the pinto beans overnight in a saucepan of cold water. Drain them well, then put them in a pan and cover with fresh water. Bring them to the boil and boil for ten minutes, then reduce the heat and cook them at a steady simmer for 2 hours. When they are soft, drain them.

Pour the vegetable oil into a pan over a medium heat. Sweat the onions and celery for five minutes, constantly stirring to stop them from browning. Then add the chilli and garlic and stir them through. Add the spice mix and allow it to cook briefly, then add the beans, tomatoes and the stock. Cover the pan and cook on a medium heat for 30 minutes.

Risotto of asparagus, dolcelatte, artichoke, petit pois and mint topped with a baked herb ricotta cake

GF

We make many different types of risotto in the restaurant but this is a favourite of ours – especially lovely with freshly picked petit pois and asparagus.

Serves 6

50g butter
4 medium shallots, peeled and finely chopped
4 cloves of garlic, peeled and finely chopped
500g arborio rice
600ml white wine
900ml vegetable stock
100g dolcelatte, crumbled
100g freshly grated parmesan-style vegetarian cheese
6 marinated long-stem artichoke hearts
1 bunch of asparagus, approximately 400g
1 tsp salt
300g petit pois

For the ricotta cakes:
300g ricotta
1 egg, beaten
1 clove of garlic, finely chopped
½ nutmeg, freshly grated
2 tbsp finely chopped chives
salt and pepper to season
100g feta

Preheat the oven to 200°C/gas mark 6.

Make the ricotta cakes. Place all the ingredients, apart from the feta, in a large bowl and whisk them together, then crumble in the feta and whisk again. Now you need six 7cm diameter rings, or the equivalent, to cook the cakes; you could also use a six-hole muffin tin. Take a baking tray, line it with baking paper and then lightly oil the rings and put them on the tray, or just oil the muffin tin. Spoon the ricotta mixture equally between the rings and smooth over the tops. Place in the preheated oven for 25 minutes until set and golden brown on top.

For the risotto, melt the butter in a thick wide-based pan and add the shallots; cook them gently. After a few minutes add the garlic, stirring all the time so nothing browns. Add the rice to the pan, stirring it to make sure that the rice is coated in the butter. Then add the wine and allow the alcohol to evaporate. Keep stirring. Pour half of the stock in slowly, stirring all the time. When this reduces a little, add the crumbled dolcelatte, the parmesan, the artichoke hearts and the rest of the stock. Turn the heat down to low and stir for 20–30 minutes while the rice absorbs the stock. The rice must be cooked through but still be firm otherwise it will turn into baby food.

While the risotto is cooking, bring a pan of water to the boil and add the salt. Blanch the asparagus for 3 minutes, then drain it and put it in a bowl of iced water to refresh it. Take it out and cut each stem in three, preferably on the diagonal which looks attractive. Add these and the uncooked petits pois to the risotto about 5 minutes before the end of cooking and stir them through.

Serve the risotto topped with the ricotta cakes, and accompanied by a green salad with a sharp lemon and olive oil dressing.

Red lentil, sweet pepper and mozzarella savoury cakes, page 90

Fritters, galettes and burgers

GFO
Butternut risotto fritters with marinated roasted aubergines and chargrilled asparagus spears

The smoked cheddar cheese used in the recipe gives the risotto fritters a fantastic flavour. To make the dish even more special drizzle the plate with some basil- and chive-infused oil.

Serves 8

For the risotto fritters:
1 large butternut squash, peeled, deseeded and cut into 2cm cubes
a little olive oil
salt and pepper
50g butter
3 banana shallots, peeled and diced
3 cloves of garlic, finely chopped
1 large bunch of thyme – discard the stalks and chop the leaves
500g arborio rice
200ml white wine
750ml vegetable stock
100g finely grated parmesan-style vegetarian cheese
100g grated smoked vegetarian cheddar (or a strong vegetarian smoked cheese), grated
1 large bunch of chives, chopped
4 eggs, beaten
100g breadcrumbs (gluten-free if needed)
100ml vegetable oil

For the aubergines and asparagus:
2 medium aubergines
2 tbsp vegetable oil
salt and pepper
3 tbsp olive oil
juice and zest of 1 lemon
half a bunch of fresh thyme, stalks removed and leaves chopped finely
1 small red chilli, deseeded and roughly chopped
2 tsp cumin
1 tsp paprika
1 bunch of spring onions, finely chopped
1 large bunch of asparagus, woody end cut off
a little vegetable oil

Preheat the oven to 200°C/gas mark 6. Place the chunks of butternut squash on a baking tray, drizzle with olive oil and season with salt and pepper. Cover the tray with foil and roast the squash in the oven for 20–25 minutes.

Melt the butter in a large pan, add the shallots and gently sweat them for 2–3 minutes. Add the garlic and thyme and cook for a minute then put the rice in the pan, stirring it well so that the grains are coated in the butter. Add the wine and cook on a medium heat until the wine has been absorbed. Then add half the stock and allow the rice to cook, stirring occasionally.

Once that liquid has been absorbed, mash up the roasted butternut squash and add it to the risotto with the cheeses, the chives and the rest of the stock. Stir well and season with salt and pepper. Allow the rice to continue cooking, stirring occasionally until all the remaining liquid has been absorbed. Check the rice to make sure it is cooked through but still firm. Then spread it out on a large tray or dish so that it cools down quickly, and leave it to cool for 30 minutes.

While it is cooling, prepare the aubergines and asparagus. Top and tail the aubergines, and then cut each one into three round slices. Place them on a baking tray, drizzle with the vegetable oil, season with salt and pepper and roast in the oven for 10 minutes.

Make the marinade while they are roasting. Blend together the olive oil, lemon juice and zest, the thyme, chilli, cumin and paprika. When the aubergine pieces are cooked, put them in a dish and pour the marinade on top, then sprinkle the chopped spring onions on top of everything. Cover with foil and keep warm until needed.

When the rice is cold, divide it into sixteen equal portions and either mould them into round balls or use a ring and make discs. Dip these risotto cakes into the egg and then into the breadcrumbs. Heat the vegetable oil in a large frying pan and fry them for 2 minutes on each side to give them a golden colour, then transfer them to a baking tray and cook in the oven for 10 minutes.

Bring a pan of salted water to the boil and cook the asparagus for 3 minutes, then remove it. Cool the spears under cold running water. Heat up a griddle pan, brush the asparagus with oil and grill for a minute on each side.

To serve, put the risotto fritters on the individual plates with the vegetables alongside. Serve with a rocket and cherry tomato salad scattered with parmesan-style vegetarian cheese shavings, if you wish.

Aubergine croque monsieur with spring onion and roasted garlic mash and parsley butter

This is our take on the traditional French croque-monsieur. We serve ours with roasted garlic mash and a lemon-dressed rocket salad.

Serves 6

2 large aubergines
salt and pepper
a little olive oil
2kg red potatoes, such as Desiree
8 cloves of garlic, peeled
200ml double cream
250g salted butter, room temperature
1 bunch of spring onions, finely chopped
1 medium bunch of flat-leaved parsley
200g breadcrumbs
60g freshly grated parmesan-style vegetarian cheese
zest of 1 lemon
half a bunch of chives, finely chopped
200g smoked vegetarian cheese, cut into thin slices approximately 5cm in length
100g plain flour
2 eggs, beaten
2 tbsp vegetable oil

Preheat the oven to 180°C/gas mark 4. Take the aubergines and cut them lengthways into six slices per aubergine. Season with salt and pepper and rub both sides with a little olive oil. Spread them on a baking tray and cook in the oven for 5–7 minutes so that the aubergines are soft and half cooked, then set them aside.

Peel the potatoes, cutting the larger ones in half, and put them in a large saucepan of cold water. Bring it to the boil and simmer for 20–30 minutes until soft; drain them in a colander and allow to cool. When the potatoes have cooled, mash them by hand – or for a really smooth mash put them through a potato ricer.

Line a small baking tray with foil. Put 5 garlic cloves on it, cover tightly with another piece of foil and roast the garlic in the oven for 10 minutes until it is soft.

Gently heat 200ml of double cream in a small saucepan; don't let it boil. Add half the salted butter and allow it to melt. Mash the roast garlic and add it to the butter and cream mix, then add the mix and the spring onions to the mashed potato, and stir everything together well. Using a small blender, blend the remaining butter, parsley and three cloves of garlic. Gently warm them through in a saucepan.

Put the breadcrumbs in a bowl and add the parmesan, lemon zest, chives and a pinch of salt and mix them through. Then take two aubergine slices and put a slice of smoked cheese in between them, making an aubergine sandwich. Repeat, making 6 sandwiches. Put the flour in a bowl and beat the eggs in another. Put them next to the bowl with the breadcrumb mix in.

Take each aubergine sandwich and carefully dip it into the flour, then into the egg and finally into the breadcrumb mix so that the outside is coated on both sides. Put aside until they are all ready. Heat the vegetable oil in a frying pan and gently fry the aubergine stacks over a low heat for approximately 2–3 minutes on each side until they are golden brown. Put them on warmed plates. Serve them with the garlic mash and drizzled with the parsley butter. A rocket salad with a lemon dressing is a good accompaniment.

GFO
Puy lentil, goat's cheese and olive burgers

These are great as an addition to a summer lunch in the garden – throw them on the barbeque, perhaps – or simply as a supper for the family during the week. We like to serve them in toasted focaccia with chilli jam (see page 14), accompanied by some oven-baked potato wedges tossed in olive oil and lemon thyme, and a crisp leaf and tomato salad. This recipe will make between 6 and 8 burgers.

Serves 6–8

700ml water
375g Puy lentils
3 tbsp vegetable oil
250g onion, chopped
2 cloves of garlic, finely chopped
1 celery stick, finely chopped
1 x 250g log of goat's cheese, skinned
1 sprig of rosemary, leaves finely chopped
150g breadcrumbs (gluten-free if needed)
200g pitted black olives, roughly chopped
1 egg, beaten
1 tsp salt
freshly ground pepper

Preheat the oven to 180°C/gas mark 4. Put the cold water in a saucepan with the Puy lentils and bring to the boil. Simmer until the lentils are cooked; they should be quite soft. How long this takes will depend on how fresh the lentils are, but allow about 30 minutes. Drain any excess water off.

Heat a tablespoon of the oil in a pan and add the onions, garlic and celery. Cook on a low heat for about 10 minutes until they are soft but without any colour. Take the pan off the heat and crumble in the goat's cheese, mixing it well. Then add the rosemary and the breadcrumbs and stir them through.

Cover a baking tray with greaseproof paper. Add the chopped olives, egg, salt and pepper to the lentils and roughly blend into a paste, using a hand blender. Add the onion and cheese mix to the paste and mix it thoroughly by hand. Check the seasoning and then form the mixture into burgers. Put them on the baking tray and chill in the fridge for 15 minutes.

Put the remaining 2 tablespoons of vegetable oil in a frying pan and shallow-fry the burgers for 3 minutes on each side. Put them back on the baking tray and finish them in the oven for 10 minutes before you are ready to eat. Serve with your favourite toppings such as onions, chutneys and slices of cheese.

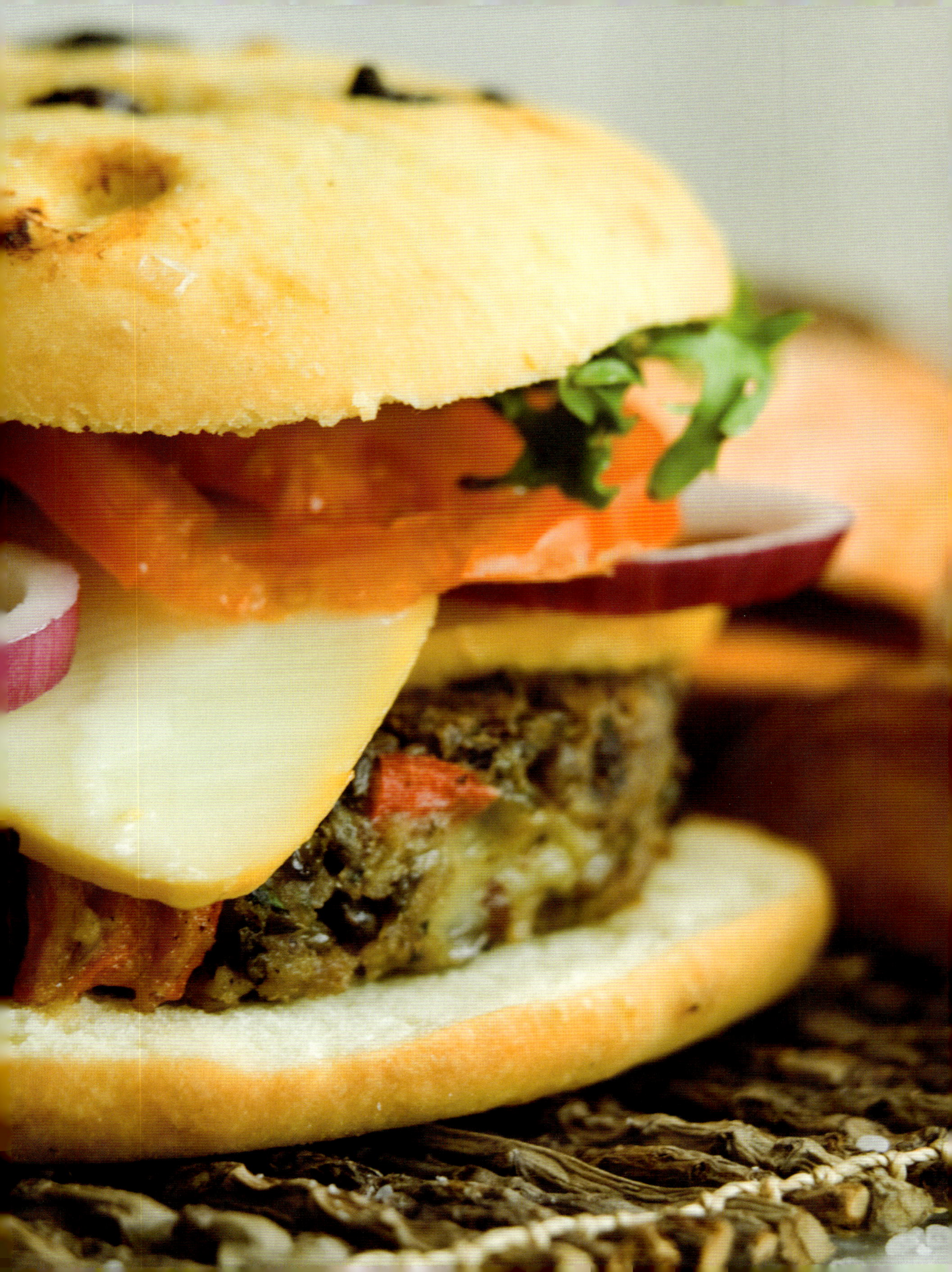

VO
Spicy lentil and sun-dried tomato burger, with a crispy aubergine steak, and potato wedges

These burgers are really easy to make and also to adapt with different ingredients; if you are vegan, for example, you would serve them with something other than the aubergine steak or simply shallow-fry in half vegetable oil, half olive oil and season. We have used Puy lentils here as they remain firmer and give the burger a much richer flavour. A good burger is tasty, succulent but at the same time can't fall to pieces the moment you try and eat it…

Makes 6 burgers

For the lentil burgers:
400g Puy lentils
1 tbsp olive oil
1 medium onion, diced
2–3 cloves of garlic, peeled and finely chopped
3 tbsp ground coriander
2 tbsp ground cumin
salt and black pepper
1 red pepper, diced
1 tsp finely chopped rosemary
1 large red chilli, (seeds optional), finely chopped
1 tbsp chopped coriander
1 tbsp plain flour
100g breadcrumbs
75g sun-dried tomatoes, finely chopped
vegetable oil, for frying

For the aubergine steaks:
1 large aubergine, topped
2 eggs
salt and pepper
100g plain flour
3 sprigs of thyme
100g breadcrumbs

Rinse the lentils under running water, then place them in a saucepan and cover with twice their volume of water. Bring to the boil and then simmer for about 15–20 minutes until they are al dente. Drain the lentils, rinse with cold water and set them aside to cool.

In a non-stick frying pan, heat the oil and sweat the onions and garlic until they are soft and translucent. Stir them so that they do not brown; that would give the burgers a burnt flavour. Add the ground coriander and cumin to the cooked onions and garlic mix and stir for about 4–5 minutes until the spices are cooked. Add this onion and garlic mixture to the cooked lentils, and season with salt and pepper to taste.

Add the rest of the burger ingredients to the lentils and mix them together well. Blend the mixture using a hand blender for a few seconds, or pulse in a food processor. It is important the mixture is not over-blended, however; you should still be able to see mainly whole lentils. Form the mixture into burger shapes either by hand or using a ring. Put them on a baking tray and keep them refrigerated until you are ready to cook them.

Prepare the aubergine. Cut it into six slices the same thickness – about 5mm. Make an egg wash by beating the eggs in a bowl, and season it with salt and pepper.

Put the flour on a plate and then add the leaves from the thyme sprigs; discard the stems. Stir them through the flour. Coat both sides of each aubergine slice with flour and thyme, dip it in the egg wash, then dip both sides of the slices in the breadcrumbs.

Now you are ready to cook both the aubergines and the burgers. Shallow-fry the burgers over a medium heat in a large frying pan for about 3 minutes each side, until crisp. Using another pan over a medium heat, shallow-fry the aubergines too, until golden and crisp on both sides – about 3 minutes on each one.

To serve, build a burger using home-made pear and plum chutney (see page 14), a slice of fresh tomato and a crispy aubergine steak. You can use regular burger buns, squares of toasted focaccia, or serve them with no bread at all. You can also accompany them with dressed salad leaves and our potato wedges…

Potato wedges

We use large baking potatoes to make wedges. They are really easy to do. Simply bake one whole potato per person for around an hour until cooked (the exact time will depend on how big the potatoes are) at 200°C/gas mark 6. Here's a good way to know they are cooked: if you stab them with a knife, the cooked potato inside will stick to the knife when you withdraw it. Cut the baked potatoes into chunky wedges and serve them as they are – or use a deep fryer and cook them at 180°C for 4–5 minutes until golden and crusty on the outside and fluffy on the inside.

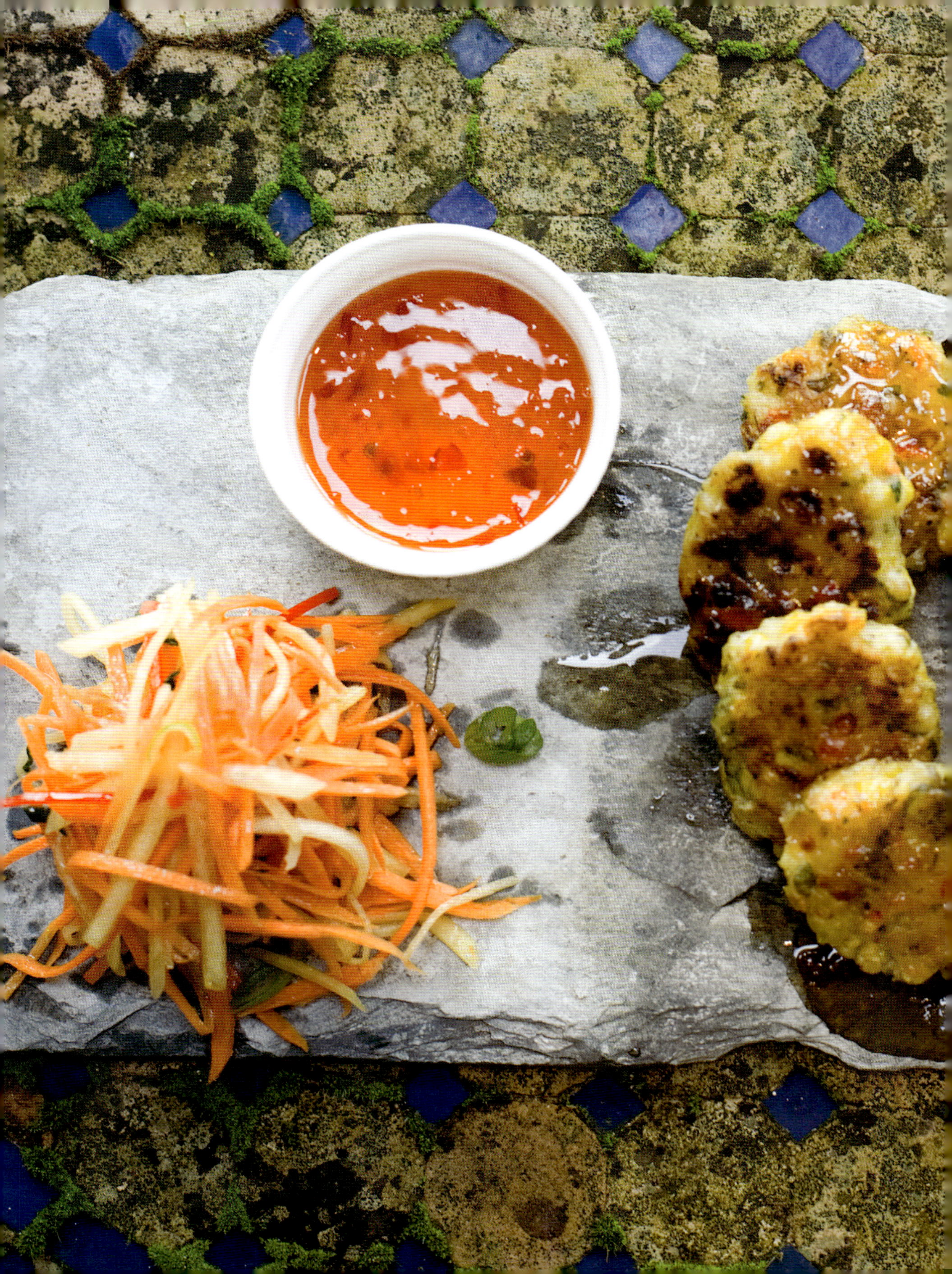

V
Thai sweetcorn fritters with a sweet chilli dipping sauce and mango salad

These fritters are delicious when served with our tom-ka soup – see page 31. Galangal can be bought in Asian and Oriental food shops, and is well worth finding for the flavour it imparts. It is similar to ginger but has a less peppery taste.

Serves 6

2 sticks of lemon grass
2 tsp chopped ginger
1½ tbsp chopped galangal
3 cloves of garlic, peeled
4 lime leaves (destalked)
half a bunch coriander, stalks only (the leaves go in the salad)
1 tbsp vegetarian Thai green curry paste
juice of 1 lime
600g frozen or canned sweetcorn, defrosted and drained
salt and pepper
2 tbsp sugar
a little plain or gluten-free flour (optional)
2 tbsp vegetable oil

For the mango salad:
1 unripe Thai mango, peeled and cut into 3mm strips
2 hard mangoes, peeled and cut into 3mm strips
2 bunches of spring onions, cut into fine diagonal strips
1 large red chilli, cut into very fine strips
1 bunch of coriander, leaves only, finely chopped
1 handful of mint leaves, finely chopped
1 handful of Thai sweet basil leaves, finely chopped

Make the mango salad by mixing all the ingredients together and set it to one side.

Cut the bases from the lemon grass sticks and remove the outer leaves. Hit the sticks with the handle of a heavy knife, crushing them, then chop them finely. Put the lemon grass, ginger, galangal, garlic, lime leaves, coriander, green curry paste and lime juice in a blender and blend them well. Put the mixture in a large bowl and add the sweetcorn. Season with salt, and stir in the sugar.

Form the sweetcorn mixture into patties; if they fail to stick together then add a small amount of flour, but use as little as possible. Heat the vegetable oil in a frying pan and cook the fritters for 3–4 minutes on each side. Serve, accompanied by the mango salad and some sweet chilli dipping sauce.

GF
Sweet potato and carrot rosti with mushroom duxelles, poached egg, creamed peas and fresh spinach

This is a great recipe for a dinner party as the rostis, mushroom duxelles and creamed peas can be prepared in advance. All you then have to do is poach the eggs and finish off the rostis in the oven. Easy! We serve the rosti with a beetroot reduction and toasted pine nuts.

Serves 6

For the rostis:
1kg large Desiree or other red potatoes, washed but not peeled
250g butter
300g sweet potatoes, peeled and grated
2 carrots, peeled and grated
3 cloves of garlic, finely chopped
1 bunch of spring onions, finely chopped
1 bunch of flat parsley, finely chopped
salt and pepper
1 tbsp vegetable oil

For the mushroom duxelles:
2 tbsp vegetable oil
2 banana shallots, peeled and finely diced
400g chestnut mushrooms, finely sliced
400g oyster mushrooms, ripped by hand into long strips
2 cloves of garlic, finely chopped
half a large bunch of parsley, chopped
2 clusters of enocchi mushrooms, roots cut off and separated by hand
salt and pepper
1 tbsp truffle oil (optional)
6 eggs
a few baby spinach leaves per person, to serve

Start preparing the rostis. Place the potatoes in large pan of cold water and bring to the boil; cover the pan and allow the potatoes to cook for 10 minutes more. Remove from the heat, drain the potatoes into a colander and cool them down under cold running water. In a small saucepan, gently melt the butter and allow it to separate, leaving the milky bit at the bottom, and retaining the clarified butter.

Peel the potatoes. Grate them into a large bowl and add the grated sweet potatoes, carrots, garlic, spring onions and parsley. Add the clarified butter carefully (leave the milky bit in the pan), season with salt and pepper and mix everything together well. Roughly divide this rosti mixture into six equal portions.

Use a 10cm metal ring to shape the rostis. Put a piece of baking paper on a tray, pop the ring on the paper and fill it with rosti mixture, pressing it into the ring. Then lift the ring off and make the next rosti, repeating until you have a total of six and have used up all of the rosti mixture. Then put the tray in the fridge for a minimum of 30 minutes to allow the rostis to set.

Now prepare the mushroom duxelles. Heat the vegetable oil in a wok or frying pan, and fry the shallots over a medium heat for 2–3 minutes without burning them. Add the chestnut and oyster mushrooms and stir frequently while they cook through – about 8–10 minutes. Then add the garlic, parsley and enocchi mushrooms and cook for a further 2 minutes. Season with salt and pepper and truffle oil, and put the pan to one side.

For the creamed peas, melt the 25g butter in a saucepan on a medium heat and sweat the shallot for 2–3 minutes. Add the garlic and leave for a minute. The add the double cream and bring almost to the boil; just before it boils add the peas and cook for 5 minutes. Take the pan off the heat and, using a hand blender, roughly blend the peas and season to taste.

Preheat the oven to 220°C/gas mark 7 when you have prepared all the elements of the meal and are ready to eat. Heat a tablespoon of oil in a frying pan and fry each rosti for 2 minutes on each side. Place them on a baking tray as they are done. When they are all fried, put the tray on the middle shelf of the oven and cook the rostis for 10 minutes until crisp and golden.

When you are ready to serve, gently heat the creamed peas and warm the mushroom duxelles through. Poach an egg per person and gently lay them on some kitchen roll until you are ready. Put a little handful of baby spinach leaves on each plate, then place the rosti on top. Put a spoonful of peas on one side of the rosti, some mushrooms on the other, and then carefully place the poached egg on top. Serve immediately.

For the creamed peas:

25g butter

1 banana shallot, peeled and finely chopped

2 cloves of garlic, finely chopped

100ml double cream

150g frozen peas

salt and pepper

Fritters, galettes and burgers

GF
Red lentil, sweet pepper and mozzarella savoury cakes

This is a gluten-free recipe, however you can use fresh breadcrumbs or plain flour instead of the gluten-free flour. Serve the cakes with your favourite herb salad and red pepper coulis.

Makes about 15–20

- 600g red lentils
- 1 large onion, chopped
- 1 bunch of spring onions, finely chopped
- 1 red pepper, peeled and chopped
- 1 yellow pepper, peeled and chopped
- 4 cloves of garlic, peeled and chopped
- a little butter for sautéing
- 350g grated mozzarella
- 80g grated parmesan-style vegetarian cheese
- 1 medium bunch of parsley, finely chopped
- salt and pepper
- 100g gluten-free flour

Put the lentils in a pan and cover them with cold water. Bring to the boil, then reduce the heat and simmer well until the lentils are cooked – about 20 minutes or so (skim the froth off the top as they cook). When the lentils are soft, drain them and then refresh them in the sieve with some cold water.

Sauté the onion, spring onion, peppers and garlic in some butter until soft – about 10 minutes. Put the lentils in a large bowl, add the sauté mix, and then the cheeses and parsley. Mix everything together well by hand and check the seasoning; stir well. When it looks thoroughly mixed, add the flour and check that the consistency is thick enough to hold together and allow you to make the patties; if not, add a little more flour but be careful and don't add a lot at once. Take pieces of the mixture, roll them into balls then gently squash them into a patty shape; they should be about 10cm in diameter and 3cm thick.

Chill them in the fridge for at least 20 minutes, and preheat the oven to 200°C/gas mark 6. When you are ready to cook, pan-fry the patties in a little butter for 3–4 minutes either side and then put them on a baking tray. Finish them off in the oven for 6 minutes.

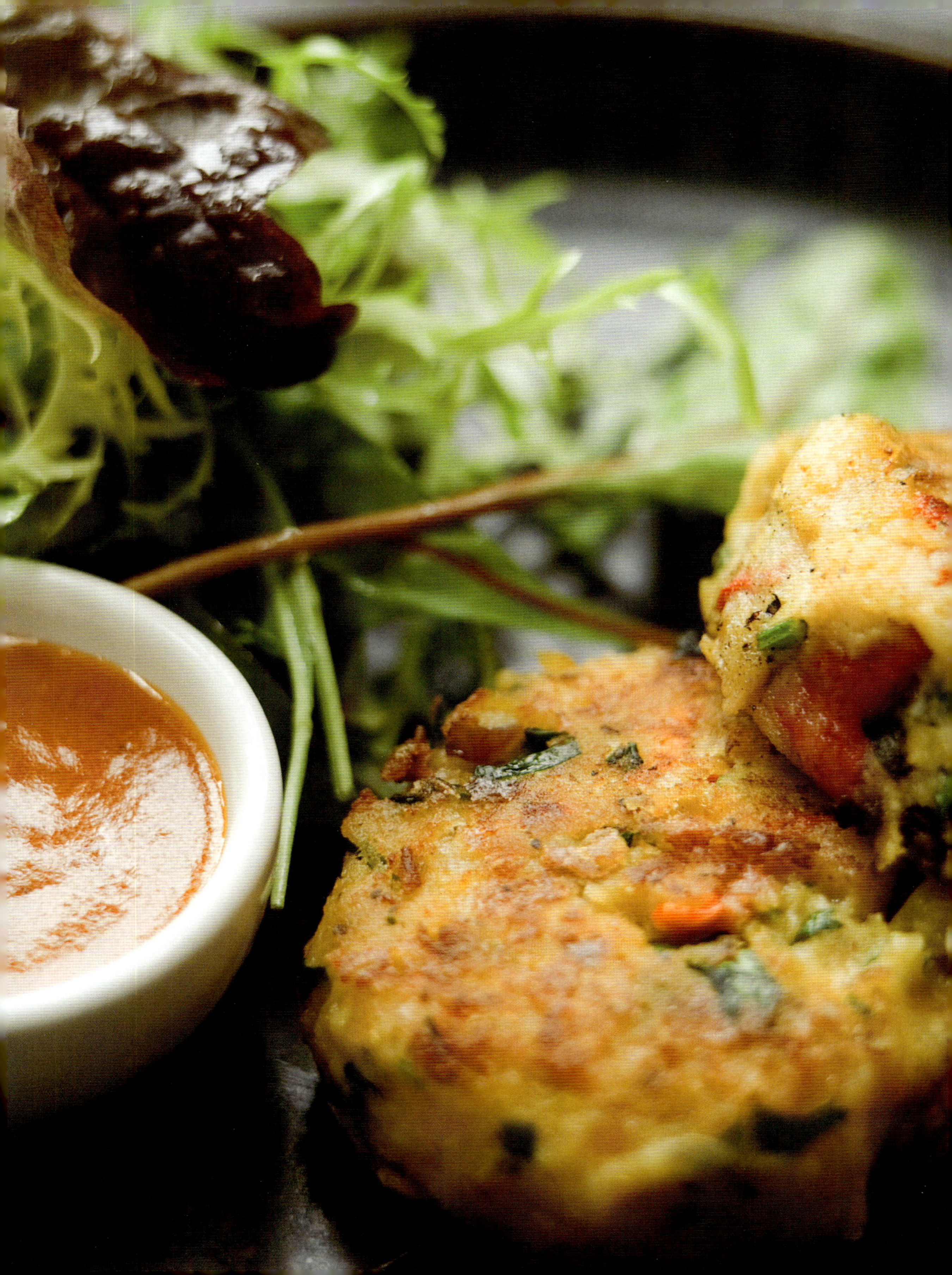

Savoury truffled sun-dried tomato and smoked cheese beignet with basil cream and roasted butternut squash

Over the years, Food for Friends has had many different beignet dishes on the menu; this is one of our favourites. This is our own savoury take on the classic French doughnut, which is made from choux pastry with a fruit filling.

Serves 8

For the beignets:
500ml cold water
250g unsalted butter, cubed
300g plain flour
7 eggs
200g smoked hard vegetarian cheese, finely grated
1 medium bunch of basil, separated into leaves and stalks (the stalks are for the sauce)
100g sun-dried tomatoes, finely chopped
4 tsp white truffle oil
salt and pepper

For the basil cream sauce:
half a medium white onion, finely chopped
4 cloves of garlic
1 tbsp olive oil
400ml double cream
100g parmesan-style vegetarian cheese
salt and pepper

For the roasted butternut squash:
4 small butternut squash
2 tbsp cumin seeds
salt and pepper
a little olive oil

Preheat the oven to 180°C/gas mark 4 and start the beignet dough. Put the 500ml of water in a large saucepan over a medium heat. Add the cubed butter to the water and bring the water to the boil, allowing the butter to melt. Then add the flour. Using a whisk, beat it furiously, combining the flour and water until the mixture comes away from the sides as a soft dough. Put the pan in a cool place and allow the dough to cool down.

Then prepare the butternut squash. Simply slice the squashes in half and remove the seeds, then put the halves on a baking tray cut side uppermost. Sprinkle with the cumin seeds, season with salt and pepper and drizzle with olive oil. Place them in the oven and cook them for about 20–25 minutes until soft right through and golden in colour. Keep them warm if they are done before you have finished making the beignets.

While they are cooking prepare the sauce and finish the beignets. Sweat the onion and garlic in the olive oil until soft. Add the basil stalks, cook gently over a low heat for 2 minutes and then add the cream. Cook for 5 minutes more, being careful that the sauce does not boil, then add the parmesan and cook for a further 3 minutes until the sauce thickens slightly. Allow the sauce to cool a little. Using a hand blender or food processor, blend the sauce to a smooth cream and season to taste. Pass through a sieve to remove any basil stalks. Return it to the saucepan over a low heat until needed.

By now the beignet dough should be cool. Add one egg at a time and mix it in, then add the next and so on. Chop the basil leaves and add them, then add the smoked cheese, the sun-dried tomatoes and the truffle oil. Mix everything well, and check the seasoning.

Whether you are using a deep-fat fryer or a pan, heat the oil to 145°C, and have a baking sheet covered with greaseproof paper ready to put the uncooked beignets on, and spread some kitchen paper out for the cooked ones.

Take two tablespoons and scoop some of the soft dough up in one spoon, then shape it into an oval quenelle using the two spoons together. Place it on the baking sheet ready to cook and repeat until all of the dough has been used.

When the oil is ready, gently cook a few at a time for 12–15 minutes so that they are golden brown. When they are ready they will start to expand. Remove them from the oil with a slotted spoon and place them on the kitchen paper to drain. Keep them warm while you cook the rest.

To serve, divide the beignets between the plates. Put half a butternut squash on each plate, and drizzle with the sauce.

To make the dish more special you can roast the butternut with some vegetarian emmental cheese. You could serve the beignets with wilted spinach and steamed broccoli or other steamed greens of your choice.

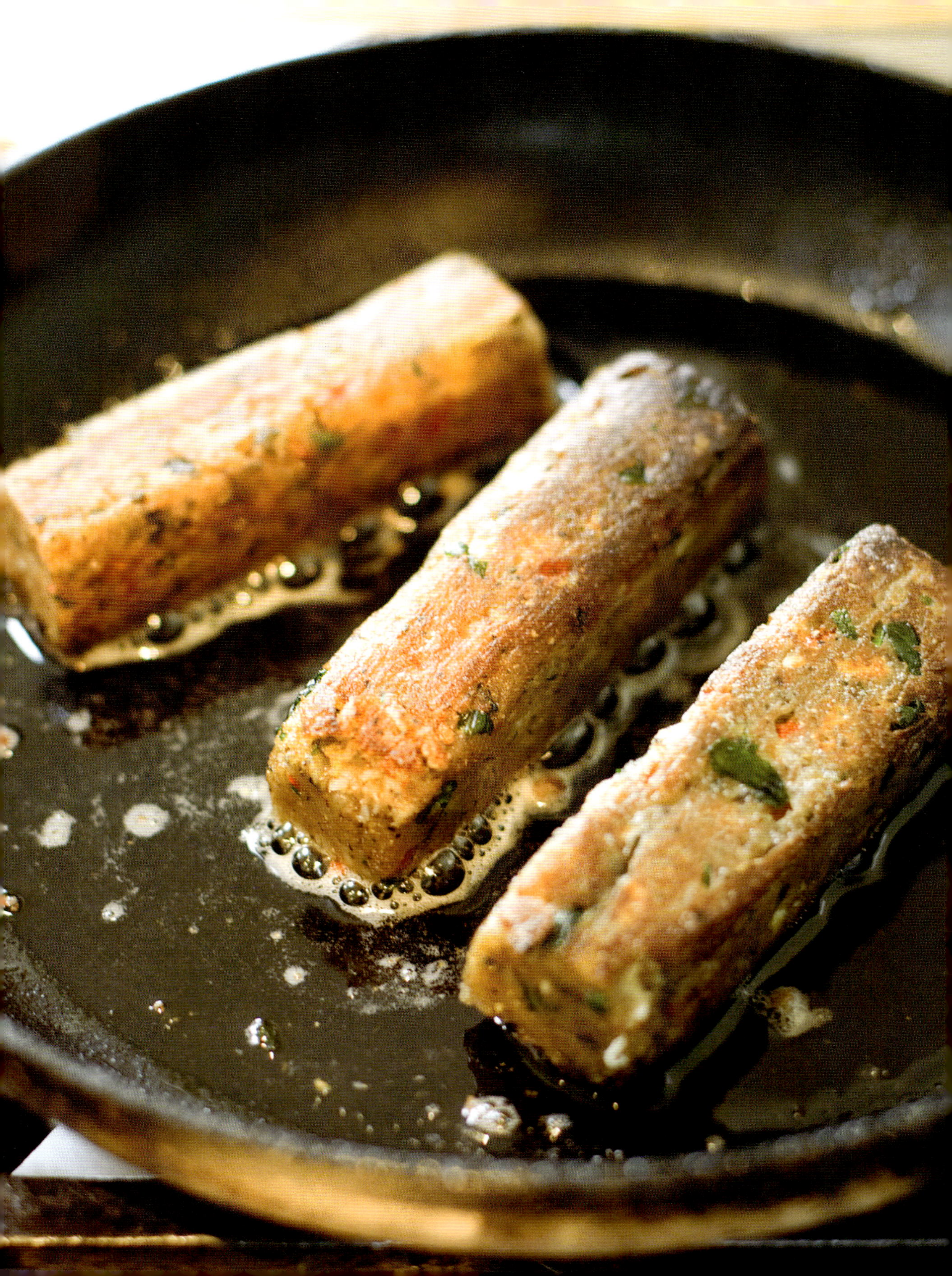

V, GFO
Snorkers not porkers

Our customers here can't get enough of our home-made sausages with creamy mash, gravy and wilted spinach. When you see how easy it is to make these sausages, we are sure you will be off experimenting with your own flavours. They are so straightforward to make and can be used in toad in the hole, with a cassoulet or simply served with mashed potato and gravy (see page 131). One thing: don't use ready-made breadcrumbs as they will be too dry. Just whiz some chunks of day-old bread very briefly in a blender, and use gluten-free bread if necessary.

Serves 8

Sun-dried tomato and black olive sausages

400g white breadcrumbs
200g sun-dried tomatoes
200g pitted black olives
6 cloves of garlic
2 tsp truffle oil
6 tbsp plain or gluten-free flour
4 tbsp vegetable oil, for frying

Preheat the oven to 200°C/gas mark 6. Blend the breadcrumbs, sun-dried tomatoes, black olives, garlic and truffle oil in a food processor. Then decant the mixture into a bowl and stir in the flour until you have a dough-like paste.

Put two layers of cling film over a chopping board. Take a quarter of the mix and line it up in a rough sausage shape along the cling film. Roll the cling film over the sausage mix and keep rolling, as though you were rolling a rolling pin, until you have a nice long sausage. Half way along, twist the cling film to separate it into individual sausages; make sure they are evenly shaped. Unwrap the cling film and set the sausages aside. Repeat with the rest of the mixture.

Heat the vegetable oil in a large frying pan and, when hot, cook the sausages for 5 minutes or until they have a nice golden colour. Then put them on a baking tray and pop them in the oven for 4 minutes to cook a little more.

Serves 4

Spinach, 'parmesan' and pine nut sausage mix
2 tbsp pine nuts
250g breadcrumbs
100g fresh baby spinach, roughly chopped
100g parmesan-style vegetarian cheese, grated
2 cloves of garlic
sprinkle of sea salt

Preheat the oven as before and toast the pine nuts for 2 minutes. Then blend them with the rest of the ingredients – but only to a coarse paste; if it's too smooth it will also be too sticky (if this happens add a tablespoon of extra breadcrumbs). Then shape and cook the sausages as before.

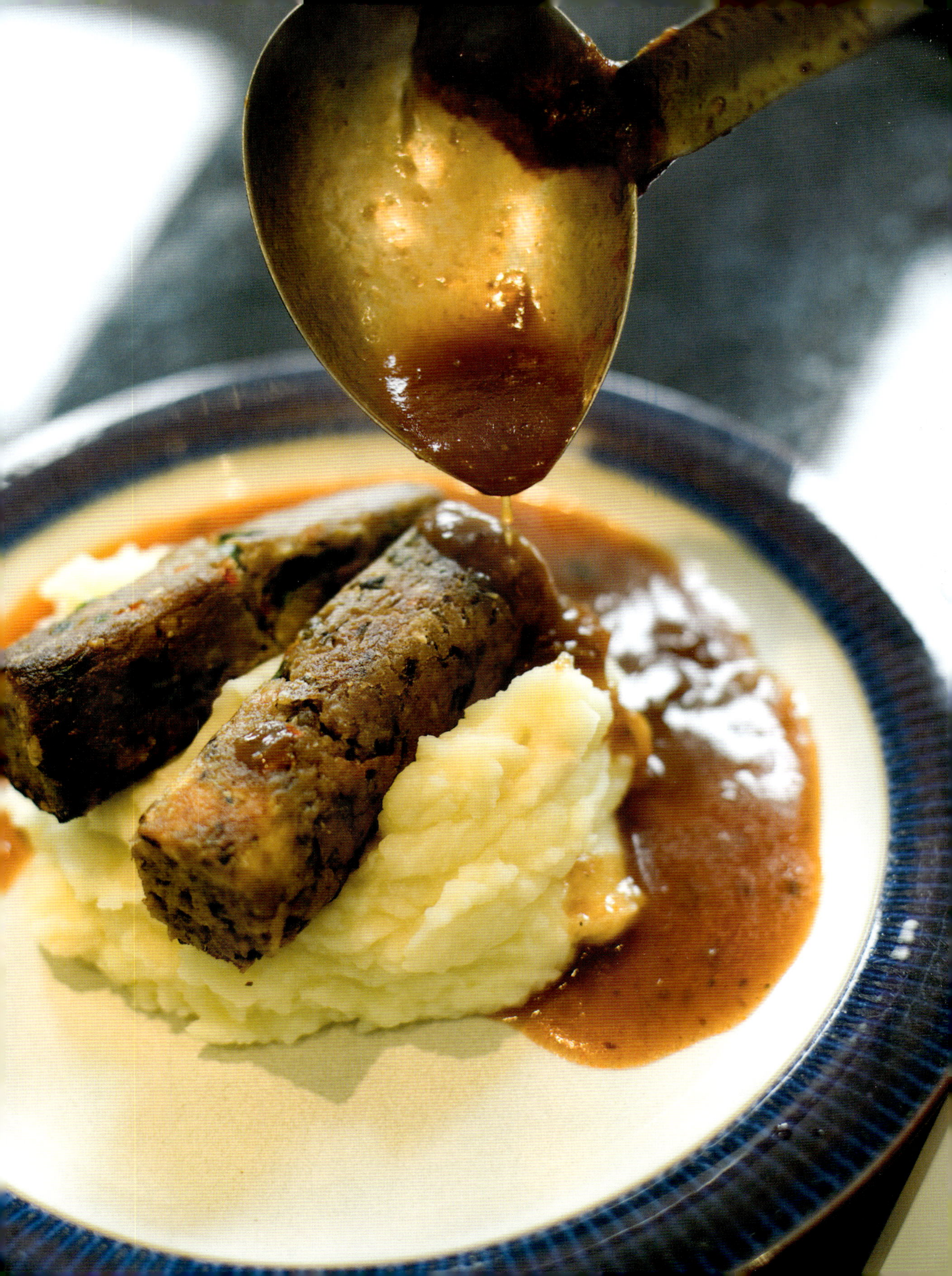

Porcini and blue cheese crispy arancini on a pumpkin galette with beetroot and chilli jam

This dish takes its influences from a classic Italian dish with a twist on the galette, and the beetroot and chilli jam cuts through the richness of the cheese and rice. There are three different components – but it's worth doing for that special occasion, as the finished dish looks spectacular. It can be prepared in advance; the arancini and galettes can be warmed through in the oven just before you need them.

Serves 4

For the arancini:
500ml boiling water
100g dried porcini or other wild mushrooms
2 tbsp olive oil
1 large white onion, finely chopped
300g arborio rice
125ml white wine
1 vegetable stock cube
120g vegetarian blue cheese, chopped up
a handful of fresh basil, roughly chopped
150g plain flour
4 eggs
3 tbsp milk
300g really dry breadcrumbs
vegetable oil for frying

For the beetroot and chilli jam:
500g white onions, finely sliced
1–2 tbsp olive oil
65g caster sugar
300ml red wine vinegar
80g fresh red chillies, roughly chopped and deseeded
375g cooked beetroot, grated

For the galettes:
50g Puy lentils
150g pumpkin, peeled, deseeded and diced
2 tbsp olive oil
salt and pepper
75g finely grated parmesan-style vegetarian cheese

Pour the boiling water on the dried mushrooms and let them soak for 15–20 minutes. Make the jam while they soak (it can also be made in advance and then warmed through a little just before you are ready to serve the meal). Sweat the onions off in the olive oil over a medium heat, and when they are soft add the sugar, wine vinegar and chillies. Turn the heat down to low and cook slowly. When there is no liquid left, add the grated beetroot and stir it through. Put it to one side.

Prepare the arancini. Drain the mushrooms, keeping the liquid to make a stock. Heat the olive oil in a large heavy-based saucepan and sauté the mushrooms and chopped onion until soft, without allowing the onions to colour. Add the rice to the pan and stir to coat it with the oil and onions for 2–3 minutes. Then add the white wine and allow it to reduce.

Crumble the vegetable stock cube into the reserved mushroom liquid and gradually pour this into the pan, stirring constantly. When the liquid has been absorbed, stir in the dolcelatte and the basil. Leave the risotto somewhere to cool down; if possible spread it out on a large plate to allow it to cool more quickly. When cold, divide it into four portions and roll them into large balls. Chill these in the fridge for 20 minutes.

Then prepare the galettes. Preheat the oven to 180°C/gas mark 4. Place a pan of salted water on to boil, and add the lentils. Cook them for 15 minutes. Put the diced pumpkin in a roasting pan, toss it with the olive oil and season with salt and pepper. Roast for 10 minutes, by which time the pumpkin should be cooked and soft. In a bowl, mix the hot pumpkin, cooked lentils and grated parmesan; season if necessary. Spread some greaseproof paper on a baking tray, shape the mixture into four round galettes and place them on the paper to cool.

When you are ready to serve, preheat the oven to 200°C/gas mark 6. Press the risotto balls down into patties. Put the flour in a bowl. Beat the eggs in another bowl and stir in the milk; put the breadcrumbs in a third bowl. Dip each patty in the flour, then in the egg mixture and finally in the breadcrumbs. Heat a generous amount of vegetable oil in a large pan and shallow fry them for 4 minutes on either side until golden brown. Put them on a baking tray.

Then put both the arancini and the galettes in the oven for 10 minutes to make them crispy. Warm up the beetroot and chilli jam while they cook. When you are ready to serve, put a galette on each plate and top it with an arancini; spoon some beetroot jam on the side.

Stuffed portabello mushrooms with pistachio pesto, sweet potato wedges and fine beans, page 105

Parcels, tarts, soufflés & stuffed veggies

V, GF
Sweet tofu pockets with mirin dressing and pickled vegetables

Tofu pockets, known as inariage, can be bought from Oriental or Asian supermarkets. The tamari is a gluten-free soy sauce. If you don't need a gluten-free option then just use light soy sauce.

Serves 6

500ml water
200g brown rice
1 tbsp vegetable oil
½ a white onion, chopped
400g oyster mushrooms, chopped
2 cloves of garlic, finely chopped
2 tbsp soy sauce or tamari
1 bunch of spring onions, finely chopped
200g butternut squash, roasted and mashed
2 tbsp mirin
salt and pepper
1 ripe avocado
4 packets of tofu pockets
mirin dressing (see page 8)

Optional garnish:
pickled ginger
enocci mushrooms

For the pickled vegetables:
1 carrot
½ cucumber
100g mouli radish
100ml white wine vinegar
100g caster sugar
100ml water

The night before, prepare the pickled vegetables. Julienne the carrot, cucumber and mouli using a mandolin. Whisk together the vinegar, sugar and water until all the sugar has dissolved. Soak the vegetables in the liquid overnight.

Put the water into a large saucepan, bring it to the boil and add the rice. Cook for 15 minutes. Drain well.

Heat 1 tablespoon of oil in a frying pan and fry the onion and mushrooms together for 5 minutes, then add the garlic, tamari or soy sauce and half the spring onions. Cook them through and then mix them with half of the cooked rice. Add the butternut mash, mirin, salt and pepper to the other half of the cooked rice, along with the remaining spring onions.

Open the tofu cases and stuff them carefully with the two types of rice using a teaspoon. Chop the avocado into 2cm cubes and place these in the top of the tofu pockets; serve immediately with mirin dressing, the drained pickled vegetables and the ginger and enocci mushrooms, if using.

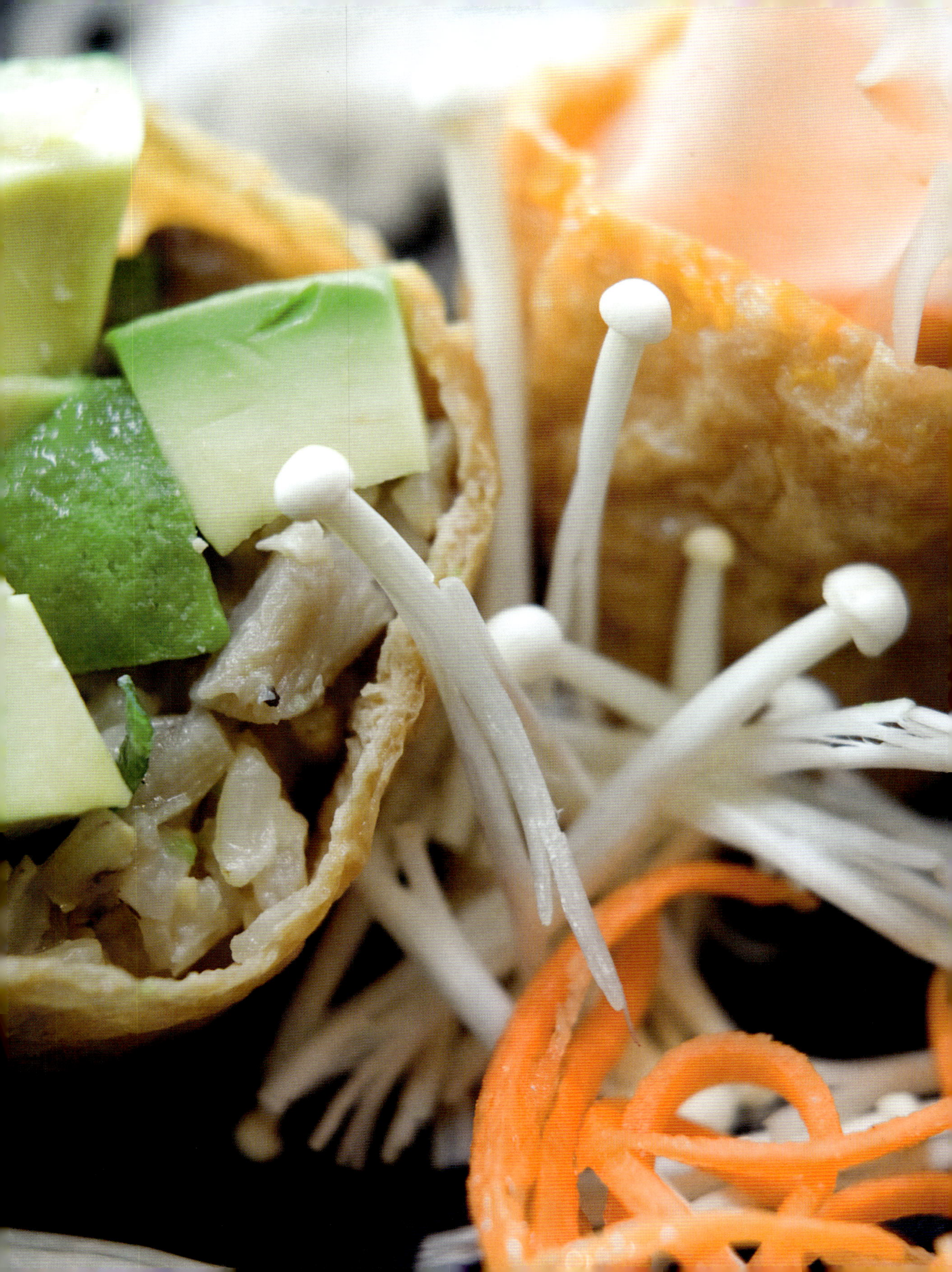

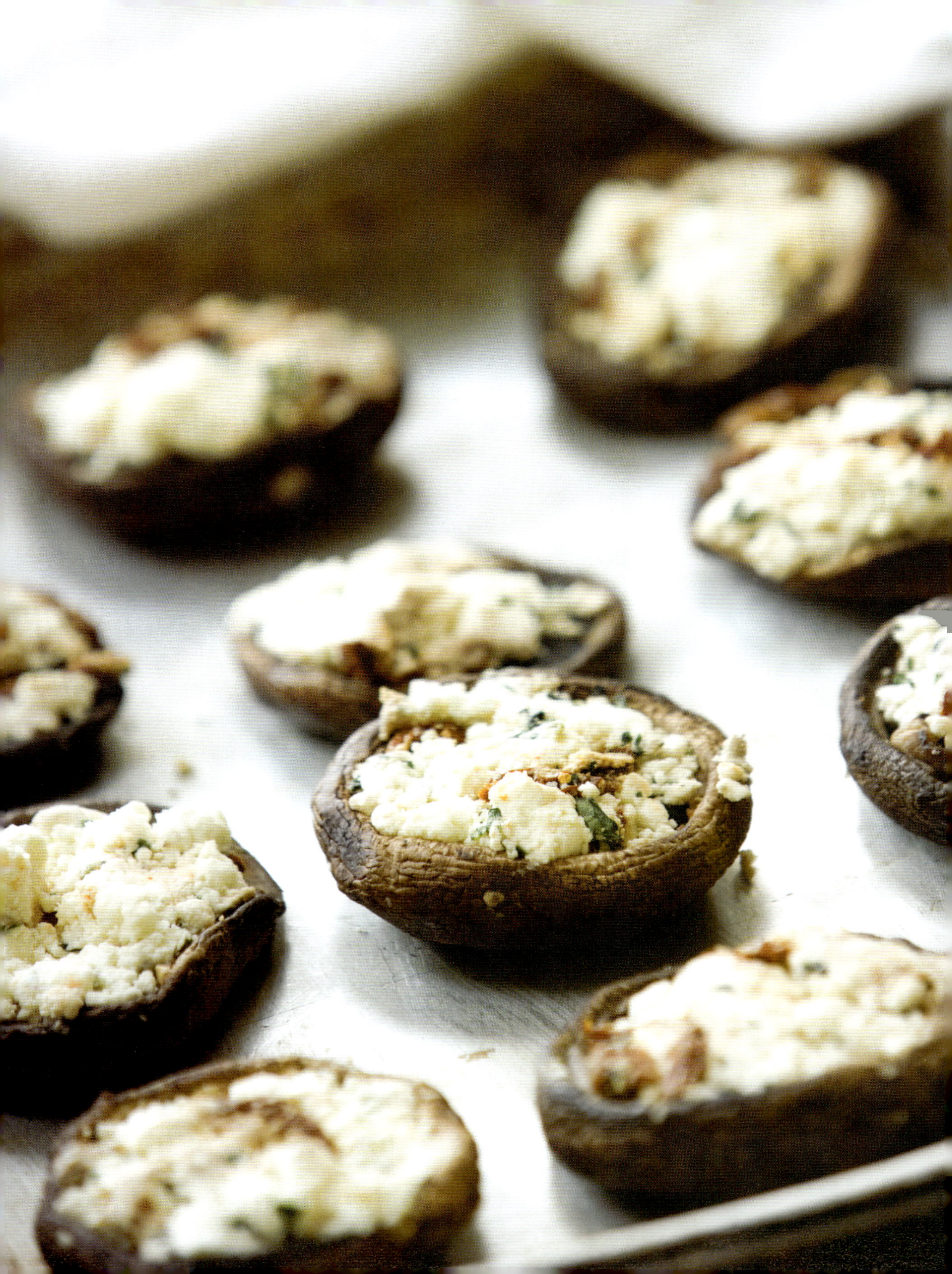

GF, N
Stuffed portobello mushrooms with pistachio pesto, sweet potato wedges and fine beans

This dish is so popular at Food for Friends that there are some customers who come to the restaurant every week for their 'portobello fix'.

Serves 6–8

4 small or medium sweet potatoes, cut into quarters
2 sprigs of rosemary, finely chopped
2 tbsp olive oil
25g butter
4 decent-sized portobello mushrooms
4 tbsp crème fraiche

For the pistachio pesto:
1 large bunch of basil leaves
50g pistachios (shelled weight)
50g parmesan-style vegetarian cheese, grated
1 clove of garlic, crushed and chopped
100ml olive oil
salt and pepper

For the feta stuffing:
300g feta, crumbled
50g pine nuts
1 medium bunch of basil, chopped
1 sprig of rosemary, leaves finely chopped
50g drained sun-dried tomatoes from a jar, very finely chopped
freshly ground black pepper

Preheat the oven to 200°C/gas mark 6. Toss the sweet potato wedges in a bowl with the chopped rosemary and olive oil and put them into an oven dish. Cook them for 25 minutes and check them a couple of times; move them around so they cook evenly.

Put all the feta stuffing ingredients in a bowl and mix them together, then put to one side. Blend all the pesto ingredients together with a hand blender (or use a mortar and pestle) and set the pesto aside as well.

As soon as the wedges are ready take them out. Cover the dish with foil and keep it somewhere warm. Increase the oven temperature to 220°C/gas mark 7.

Remove the stalks from the mushrooms. Melt the butter in a frying pan. When it is hot, fry the portobello mushrooms for 2 minutes on either side. Take them out of the pan and fill with the feta stuffing. Then place them on an oiled baking sheet and cook in the oven for 8–10 minutes, by which point they should be golden brown on the top.

To serve, put the mushrooms on warmed plates with the sweet potato wedges and vegetables of your choice – we like to serve them with steamed fine green beans. Drizzle the pesto around the mushrooms and add a spoonful of crème fraiche to each plate. Serve immediately.

VO
New potato and mushroom supreme filo parcels with marsala tomato sauce and chargrilled asparagus

If you need to make this dish dairy free substitute the single cream with soya cream and use vegan margarine instead of butter.

Serves 6–8

For the parcels:
1.2kg of mixed mushrooms, such as chestnut, portobello, oyster
400g new potatoes, chopped into wedges
400g red onion, cut into slices about 1.5cm wide
half a medium bunch of fresh thyme, leaves finely chopped
half a medium bunch of fresh parsley, finely chopped
2 sprigs of rosemary, leaves finely chopped
1 tsp piri-piri spice
1 tbsp olive oil
salt and pepper
2 tbsp vegetable oil
1 banana shallot, finely diced
4 cloves of garlic, finely chopped
50ml single cream (or soya cream)
18 sheets of ready-rolled filo pastry
4 tbsp melted butter (or vegan margarine)

For the marsala tomato sauce:
1 tbsp olive oil
1 large onion, finely chopped
4 cloves of garlic, finely chopped
1 tsp garam masala
100ml marsala wine
400g fresh ripe tomatoes, chopped
salt and pepper

Preheat the oven to 180°C/gas mark 4. Prepare the mushrooms: chop chestnut mushrooms and the like, pull oyster mushrooms into long strips. Take a large pan of salted water and boil the potato wedges. Cook them for 20 minutes, then drain and place in a large bowl.

Add the red onion slices to the bowl with the thyme, parsley, rosemary, piri-piri and a drizzle of olive oil. Season with salt and pepper and mix well. Tip them into a baking tray and roast in the oven for 10 minutes, until the potatoes and red onion are cooked through and golden.

Meanwhile, heat the oil in a pan and fry the shallot for 2–3 minutes, then add the garlic and the prepared mushrooms. Stir continuously, allowing the mushrooms to soften and cook through for 10 minutes. Then take the pan off the heat and stir in the cream or soya cream. Season with salt and pepper. Combine the mushroom mix with the potato mix in a large bowl and stir them together well.

For each parcel you will need 3 pieces of filo pastry approximately the same size as A4 paper. Take the first sheet, brush the edges with the melted butter or margarine, then place the second across it to make the shape of a cross and brush its edges with melted margarine. The third sheet needs to be placed diagonally across the other two sheets. Brush all the edges with the melted margarine.

Place approximately 4 tablespoons of the mixture in the middle of the filo pastry, pull up two opposite corners into the middle and then repeat with the other two corners. Make a little twist at the top to hold it in place. Repeat to make a total of 6 parcels. Place them on a greased baking tray. Put the parcels in the oven for 15 minutes so that the filo pastry is golden and crispy.

To make the sauce, heat the oil in a pan and sweat the onion in it until soft. Add the garlic and cook for 2–3 minutes before adding the garam masala and cooking it while stirring for 2 minutes. Add the marsala wine and allow the alcohol to burn off before adding the chopped tomatoes. Reduce the heat to low and cook for 12 minutes. Season with salt and pepper. If you like use a blender to make a smooth sauce.

Serve with chargrilled asparagus spears and the marsala tomato sauce.

V, GF
Baked tomatoes stuffed with paella rice

Serves 4

8 medium beef tomatoes, ripe but firm
half a green pepper, deseeded and pith removed, coarsely chopped
4 cloves of garlic
a large pinch of crushed dried chilli flakes
a handful of flat-leaf parsley leaves
1 tsp Spanish paprika
1 tsp saffron threads, ground in a pestle and mortar and steeped in 1 tbsp boiling water
125ml olive oil
75g paella rice
sea salt and pepper

Preheat the oven to 180°C/gas mark 4.

Take the stalks off the tops of the tomatoes. Then, to make little lids, slice horizontally about a fifth of the way down the tomatoes. Do not throw the lids away but put them aside for later. Using a teaspoon, carefully scoop out the insides of the tomatoes and place in a bowl. Put the 8 hollow tomatoes in a roasting tray that will allow them to snuggle closely together.

Put the green pepper, garlic, chilli, parsley, paprika and saffron with its water in a food processor, then pulse until all the ingredients are evenly but coarsely chopped. Now add the tomato pulp and 100ml of the olive oil and process again until the mixture is rather sloppy.

Put the rice into the bowl that held the tomato pulp and then pour the sloppy tomato mix over the rice. Mix well and season with sea salt to taste. Leave it to soak for 45 minutes, stirring occasionally.

Fill the tomatoes with the rice mixture, and make sure you get lots of the liquid in them so they stay moist – it doesn't matter if they overflow slightly. If you have any rice mixture left it can be cooked alongside.

Put the lids back on the tomatoes and then drizzle them with the remaining olive oil. Bake in the oven for about 45 minutes. Turn the heat down a little if they start to brown too quickly, but they should be brown and blistered when ready. Taste the rice to make sure that it is cooked enough.

When serving, remember to spoon the juices and oil over the tomatoes just beforehand.

If you want to make a more elaborate meal serve with marinated long-stem artichokes and a roasted aubergine and red pepper omelette.

Pumpkin and caramelised shallot tarte tatin

Serves 8

16 medium banana shallots, peeled
100ml olive oil
2 tbsp balsamic vinegar
50g soft dark brown sugar
salt and pepper
1 small pumpkin (about 1.5kg) peeled, deseeded and diced into 1.5cm cubes
1 pack ready-rolled puff pastry
50g butter
2 egg yolks, beaten

Preheat the oven to 180°C/gas mark 4. Put the shallots in a deep baking tray. Scatter them with half the oil, the balsamic vinegar and brown sugar and season with salt and pepper; mix well. Cover the tray with foil and bake for 30 minutes. Then remove the foil and bake them for another 5 minutes. Allow them to cool down.

While the shallots are cooking, place the diced pumpkin and the rest of the oil and some salt and pepper in another baking tray and cover that with foil too. Put it in the oven as well, and bake for 20 minutes. Allow the pumpkin to cool down.

You will need 8 tatin pans or a large Yorkshire pudding tray (one which is shallow and wide). Lightly flour a clean surface and roll out the puff pastry to 5mm thick. Cut out 8 circles to fit in the tatin pans or a line the depressions of the Yorkshire pudding tray. Cut the butter into 8 pieces and put one piece in each pan. Put the caramelized shallots on top, follow them with the roasted pumpkin and finally cover with the puff pastry. Then brush the beaten egg over the top of the pastry to stop it burning.

Bake in the oven for 25 minutes; turn them upside-down to serve, accompanied by some rocket with shaved parmesan-style vegetarian cheese scattered on top.

To make this dish a little more sophisticated we suggest making some goat's cheese and basil pesto quenelles which can be served on top of the tartes tatins and then drizzled with red pepper sauce (page 3). To make the quenelles blend 160g goat's cheese log, 4 tsps basil pesto (page 7) and one clove of garlic together in a food processor for 2 minutes. Using two teaspoons shape the quenelles and then gently place them on top of the tartes tatins.

Parcels, tarts, soufflés & stuffed veggies

Portobello mushroom pie with spinach and smoked mozzarella

These little pies are really cute and are both simple and quick to make. If you wish, you can make the pastry cases and salad in advance, and cook the potatoes beforehand too. Then, just before you want to eat, pan-fry the fillings, finish the pies and warm them through in the oven.

Serves 6

3 packets ready-rolled puff pastry (30cm x 22.5cm)
50g butter
1kg baby new potatoes
a little herb or olive oil
salt and pepper
1 large bag of mixed baby salad leaves
50g almonds, toasted for 5 minutes until golden
3 beetroot, cooked and peeled
balsamic dressing (see page 8)
6 large portobello mushrooms, sliced
3 cloves of garlic, finely diced
150g baby spinach
450g smoked mozzarella, cubed

Preheat the oven to 190°C/gas mark 5. Lightly grease and line a large baking tray with baking paper. Melt half the butter over a gentle heat.

Take the ready-rolled pastry sheets and measure out a first square, 14cm by 14cm. Then inside that square cut another slightly smaller square, 12cm by 12cm but without completely cutting through two facing corners. Brush the outside edge lightly with melted butter. Take one of the outside corners and fold it over diagonally to line up with the inside corner of the square; this will give you two little twists of pastry on the other corners – the photographs will help. Then repeat this again from the opposite side, so that it folds over itself again and you have a box shape. Brush it with melted butter and place it carefully on the baking tray. Repeat until you have 6 boxes. If you want lids for your boxes, cut six little squares 7cm x 7cm to be the tops of the pies. Brush them with melted butter too, and place them on the baking tray. Put the pie cases in the oven for 15 minutes or until they are golden brown.

Next, put the new potatoes in a pan of cold water, bring to the boil and cook for 20–25 minutes until they have cooked through. When they are done, drain them thoroughly and put them in a bowl. Drizzle them with a little herb or olive oil and season with salt and pepper.

Mix the salad leaves with the toasted almonds and place on individual plates or in a large bowl. Just before serving the pies, slice the beetroot into wedges and put them on top of the leaves. Drizzle the salad with some balsamic dressing.

Take a frying pan and melt the rest of the butter over a medium heat. Sauté the mushrooms with the garlic and then add the baby spinach leaves and allow them to wilt. Then add the mozzarella and cook for 2 minutes until it is slightly melted. Spoon this mixture into the pastry cases and warm them through in the oven for 5 minutes. Serve with the beetroot salad and new potatoes.

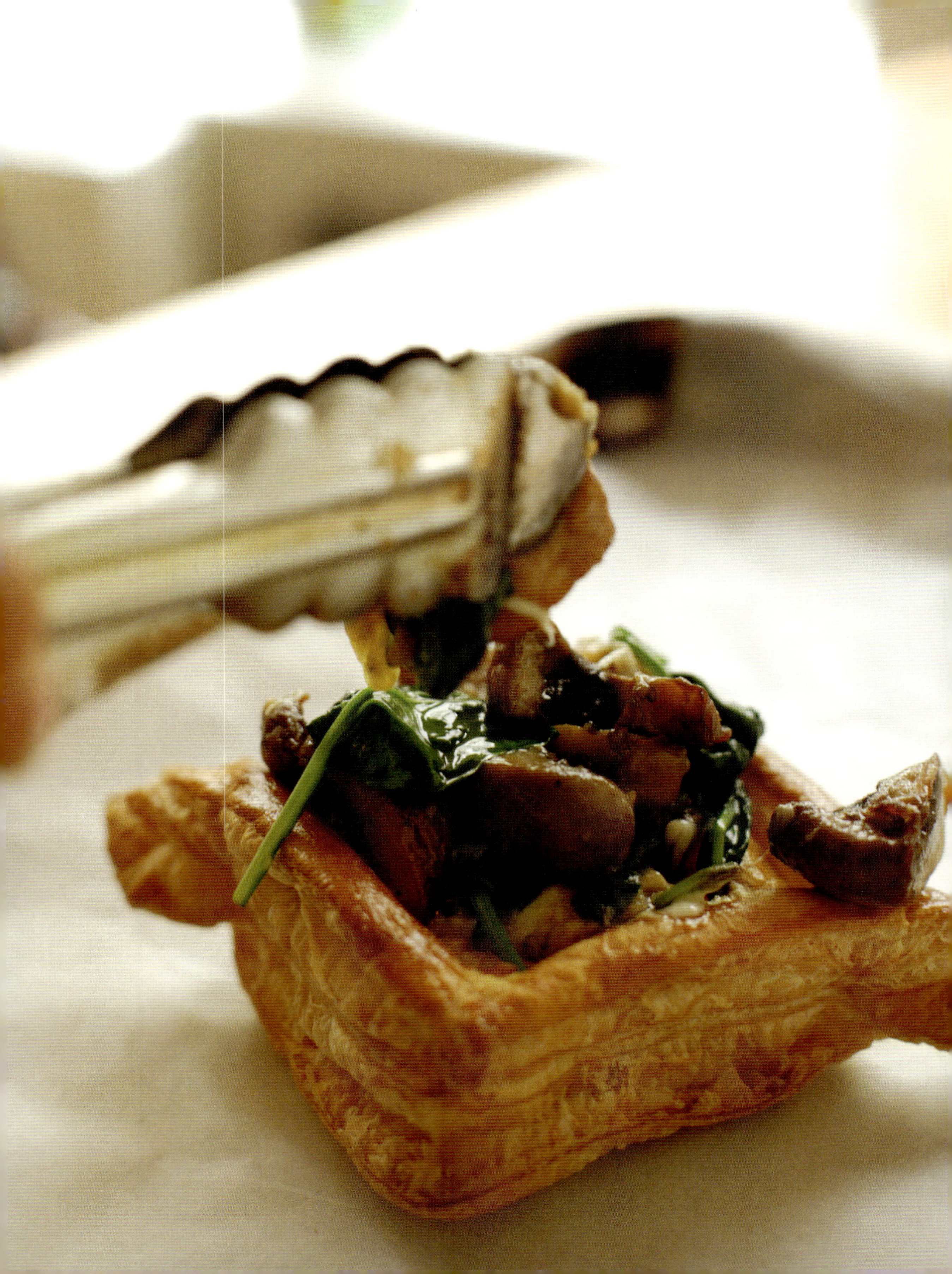

Sweet potato, spinach and dolcelatte pie

Makes one large pie, with 8–10 slices

2 medium onions, finely chopped
5 cloves of garlic, finely chopped
100g celery, finely chopped
100g butter
200ml double cream
350g dolcelatte
salt and pepper
450g sweet potato, peeled
a little vegetable oil
2 large ready-rolled sheets of puff pastry (or 500g puff pastry)
1 egg, whisked in a bowl
125g baby spinach leaves
100g parmesan-style vegetarian cheese (optional)

Preheat the oven to 200°C/gas mark 6. Put a pan over a medium heat and sweat the onions, garlic and celery in the butter for 10 minutes until soft. Stir in the cream and, just before it begins to boil (don't let it actually boil), add the dolcelatte. Lower the heat and season with salt and pepper. Simmer and allow the sauce to thicken.

Using a mandolin or food processor, slice the sweet potato into 3mm thick ribbons. Bring a pan of water to boil and blanch the ribbons for three minutes. Drain them and put to one side.

Get a pie tin or ovenproof dish about 35cm x 25cm in size, with a removable base if possible, and grease it with a little vegetable oil.

Take a sheet of puff pastry (or roll out the block). Shape it into the bottom and up the sides of the dish, allowing for shrinkage. Using a fork, prick the pastry all over to stop it puffing up. Now it needs to be baked blind. Use a piece of baking paper and drape it over the dish, overlapping the edges. Fill it with baking beans or lentils right to the top, then close the paper over the beans. Bake in the oven for 15 minutes. Take it out of the oven, remove the hot baking beans or lentils and take off the paper. Brush the pastry with the beaten egg and put it back in the oven for 5 minutes or until hard.

To make the pie, tidy the edges of the pastry with a sharp knife so they are straight. Place a layer of sweet potato ribbons on the bottom, then a generous ladle of cheese sauce. Then a layer of baby spinach, another of sweet potato and the final layer of sauce. Take the second sheet of pastry and drape it over the top, cut it to shape and pinch the edges together. Make some little slits in a nice pattern on the top to allow the steam to come out, brush it with beaten egg and sprinkle some parmesan over the top, if desired. Put the pie into the oven for 25–30 minutes, and serve hot.

We like to accompany this pie with simple steamed green beans and roasted vine tomatoes. Ten minutes before the pie is due to come out of the oven, put some baby on-the-vine tomatoes on a baking tray. Drizzle them with olive oil, add a sprinkle of sea salt and pop in the oven for ten minutes. They will be ready at the same time as the pie.

Double-baked goat's cheese soufflés with broccoli bake and pan-fried garlic spinach

These are double-baked soufflés which are great — it means that you can make them in advance and then, just before you need them, bake them for the second time.

Serves 6

For the soufflés:
80g butter
60g plain flour
350ml warm milk
1 x 75g log of goat's cheese, chopped
4 egg whites
3 egg yolks
1 tbsp grated parmesan-style vegetarian cheese
2 tbsp freshly chopped parsley
salt and pepper
200ml double cream
500g baby spinach
a little garlic oil

For the broccoli bakes:
1 large head of broccoli, roughly chopped
330ml double cream
2 cloves of garlic, finely chopped
a handful of parsley, finely chopped
150g parmesan-style vegetarian cheese, grated – plus a little for sprinkling on top
freshly ground pepper

Preheat the oven to 180°C/gas mark 4. Use 20g of the butter to grease six 8.5cm diameter ramekins generously, then put them to one side.

Melt the rest of the butter in a small pan, add the flour and stir it in to make a roux. Slowly add the milk, stirring continuously until it thickens and becomes a smooth white sauce. Take the pan off the heat, add the goat's cheese and mix until smooth. Put the pan on the side to cool for 5 minutes.

Place the egg whites in a bowl and whisk them by hand until white and creamy — but not like a foam.

Add the egg yolks and parmesan to the white sauce, and pour it into a large jug. Carefully fold in the egg whites with a metal spoon. Add the parsley, season with salt and pepper and stir them through very gently. Pour the mixture equally into the buttered ramekins. Place the filled ramekins on a deep baking tray and then fill the tray a third of the way up with boiling water. Transfer it to the oven and bake for about 20 minutes or until the soufflés are puffed and golden.

When they are out of the oven, allow them to cool for 5 minutes. Then, using a small sharp knife, loosen the edges and tip the soufflés out. Don't worry if they come out in pieces; just put them back together carefully. Place them on a tray and put them in the fridge until needed.

Now prepare the broccoli. Put all of the bake ingredients in a saucepan and cook them over a gentle heat for 10–15 minutes; do not boil. Either spoon the mixture into individual ramekin dishes or into one oven dish. Sprinkle with a little extra parmesan and grind some fresh black pepper on top.

When you are ready to serve, take the soufflés out of the fridge. Dip them in the double cream, place them on a baking tray and bake them again for 10–15 minutes or until golden and puffed up. The broccoli bakes need to go into the oven at the same time, also for 10–15 minutes, until the tops are golden brown.

While they are cooking, pan-fry the baby spinach for 2–3 minutes in a little garlic oil (or crush a clove of garlic with some olive oil). Put some spinach on each plate and top with the soufflé and the broccoli bake.

A thali, which could be created using a selection of recipes in this chapter

Big pots and slow cooking

GF, VO
Spicy potato, butternut squash, pea and paneer curry, with orange-scented rice

One morning, while we were cooking this recipe in the restaurant, the telephone rang. It was a member of staff from the restaurant opposite, saying that her general manager had asked if we could send some of whatever we were cooking over. How's that for a compliment?

Feel free to change the ingredients around with this recipe; you could use any root vegetable, just make sure that it has the same texture as the one you are replacing – if you use sweet potato the curry will have a sweeter flavour.

Serves 8

- 100ml vegetable oil
- 3 large onions, chopped
- 4 red chillies, finely chopped
- 10 cloves of garlic, finely chopped
- 2 tsp ground cumin
- 5 tsp fenugreek seeds
- 2 tsp mixed sweet spice
- 1 tsp turmeric
- 1 tsp fennel seeds
- 2 x 400g tins of chopped tomatoes
- 1 tbsp salt
- 1 large bunch of fresh coriander, coarsely chopped (including stalks)
- 1kg butternut squash, peeled and cubed into 1.5cm pieces
- 1.25kg potatoes, peeled and chopped into 3cm cubes
- 500g garden peas
- 250g paneer cheese, cubed

Heat the oil in a large deep saucepan and sweat the onions slowly over a low heat for 10 minutes. Add the red chillies and garlic. Using a mortar and pestle, mix all of the spices together, and then add them to the pan, mixing thoroughly so the spices really cook through.

Add the tinned tomatoes, the salt and half the coriander, stir them in and continue to cook. It will taste salty at this stage as the vegetables have not yet been added – they will counteract this.

Peel and deseed the butternut squash, and cut the flesh into 1.5cm cubes. Add these to the curry base in the pan, and cook for another 20 minutes. Then peel the potatoes, add them to the curry and continue to cook for another 15 minutes (don't add them at the same time as the squash; they will cook more quickly and turn to mush).

Add the peas 10 minutes before serving and, while they are cooking through, pan-fry the paneer cubes in a little oil and then stir them into the curry. Add the rest of the coriander right at the end. For a vegan version pan fry cubes of firm-textured silken tofu and add them to the curry at the end with the remainder of the coriander.

This is delicious served with orange-scented rice.

Orange-scented basmati rice

3 tsp groundnut oil

1 medium onion, peeled and finely chopped

550g white basmati rice

1.2 litres boiling water

2 rounded tsp salt

a handful of flaked almonds

1 orange, the grated zest and carefully peeled segments

1 tbsp of chopped coriander

Heat a large frying pan on a medium heat, then add the oil and onion and let it cook for 3–4 minutes, until slightly brown.

Add the rice and stir the grains so that they are coated in the oil. Then add the boiling water and the salt and stir it through once only. Cover the pan with a lid. Turn the heat to the lowest setting and do not open the lid or touch the rice for about 10–12 minutes.

After this time, uncover the pan and tilt it to see if there is any liquid; if there is, put it back on the heat for another minute. If there is not, the rice is ready. Remove the lid and cover the pan with a clean tea towel for 10 minutes before serving to allow the rice to steam through. Then transfer it to a warmed serving dish and fluff it lightly through with a fork. Sprinkle with the almonds and orange zest, and decorate it with the orange segments and coriander.

Big pots and slow cooking

V, GF
Malaysian vegetable curry, with steamed jasmine rice

This recipe has been on and off the menu at Food for Friends since we have owned the restaurant. It originally came from Friday, Jane's stepfather, who is Malaysian; it was one of the first things she was taught to cook. It is really easy to change the vegetables – but if you do, make sure you add them at the right time of cooking. For instance, if you wanted to exchange the carrots for frozen peas, then you would add the peas right at the end as they only take a couple of minutes to cook.

Serves 8 hungry people

4 tbsp vegetable oil
4 very large onions, peeled and diced
5 tbsp ground cumin
5 tbsp ground coriander
3 tbsp mustard seeds
2 tsp salt
2 tbsp ground almonds
2 star anise
3–4 bay leaves
3–4 curry leaves
1 large cinnamon stick
350ml water
4–5 whole lemon grass sticks (left whole)
150g sultanas
150g dried apricots (optional)
2 big pieces of root ginger, peeled and grated
6 cloves of garlic, peeled and grated or finely chopped
1 large bunch of coriander, finely chopped
4 x 400ml tins of coconut milk
800g carrots, peeled and chopped into diagonal chunks
500g aubergine, cut into large chunks
400g potatoes, peeled and chopped
400g courgettes, cut into diagonally sliced chunks
80g okra (optional)
400g frozen peas

Steamed jasmine rice

2 tsp vegetable oil
2 cloves of garlic, finely chopped
800g jasmine rice
2 tsp salt
a medium bunch of coriander, leaves chopped

Heat the oil in a large deep saucepan with a lid and sweat the onion until soft. Add all of the spices and leaves and the water and cook gently. Stir the pan; do not allow the spices to stick to the bottom.

Now add the lemon grass, sultanas, apricots, ginger and garlic and give it a really good stir to combine everything.

Add half the coriander and two tins of coconut milk, mix them in well and allow the curry to colour deeply and develop into a fragrant stock, which will take another 10 minutes on a low heat. Then add the carrots, aubergine and potatoes, give another quick stir and put the lid on the pan. Cook the curry for 20 minutes, then add the courgettes and the rest of the coconut milk, stir, and cover the pan again. Cook for another 15 minutes; after 10, stir in the okra if you are using it. Just before serving, stir in the peas and the rest of the coriander. Serve with jasmine rice.

Heat the oil in a large pan and gently cook the garlic, but do not let it brown. Stir the rice into the garlic and oil, so that the rice is coated. Then pour cold water over the rice until it is 2cm above the level of the rice (as a quick measure, that's about one thumb joint). Add the salt and stir to make sure the rice is not stuck to the bottom of the pan.

Increase the heat. When the water starts to boil, reduce the temperature to the lowest possible level, put a lid on the pan and allow the rice to steam for 30 minutes.

Stir the coriander through the rice just before serving; it gives a lovely fresh aroma.

V
Food for Friends vegetable tagine, with herby couscous

Ideally this dish is best served in individual tagine dishes or in a large one with a lid that can be brought to the table – however, any clay or ceramic ovenproof dish will do if it's covered with foil. The important thing is to use the dish at the table, as by changing to another you will lose some of the flavour; it will also cool down a lot more quickly. The domed lid of a tagine is there to collect the steam, allowing it to condense back into the stew and stop the dish from drying out.

Serves 4

- a little vegetable oil
- 2 red onions, peeled and chopped
- 2 celery sticks, chopped
- 4 cloves of garlic, finely chopped
- 2 tbsp tomato purée
- 2 litres vegetable stock
- salt and pepper
- 4 carrots, peeled and chopped into small chunks
- 1 small butternut squash, peeled, deseeded and chopped
- 1 sweet potato, peeled and chopped
- 8 new potatoes, chopped in half
- 16 dried apricots or prunes (or a mixture of both)
- 4 cinnamon sticks
- zest and juice of 1 lemon
- 4 tsp paprika
- 1 large bunch of parsley, chopped
- 1 large bunch of coriander, chopped
- 1 tsp brown sugar (or 4 tsp honey for a non-vegan version)

Preheat the oven to 150°C/gas mark 2.

Heat the vegetable oil in a large pan, and sweat the onions and celery. When they are soft, add the chopped garlic and cook for another 2–3 minutes. Then add the tomato purée and cook for another minute. Add the stock, bring it to the boil and allow to simmer for 10 minutes. Take the pan off the heat and season with salt and pepper.

Take the four individual tagines or dishes (or one large dish) and add the carrots, butternut squash, sweet potato, new potatoes, apricots or prunes, and cinnamon sticks. Sprinkle with the lemon zest and juice, paprika, parsley, coriander and brown sugar or honey, and then add the stock mixture.

Place the lids of the tagines on top, or alternatively use foil. Cook slowly in the oven for 1½ –2 hours, by which time all of the vegetables should be cooked through. Bring straight to the table, and remove the covers. Serve with herby couscous.

Herby couscous

200g couscous

3 tbsp olive oil

1 litre vegetable stock, warm

100g flaked almonds

3 spring onions, finely chopped

3 plum tomatoes, skinned, deseeded and chopped

1 large bunch of parsley, finely chopped (discard the stalks)

100g raisins

1 small bunch of fresh mint, chopped (discard the stalks)

1 small bunch of coriander, chopped (discard the stalks)

salt and pepper

Place the couscous in a large bowl, add the olive oil and mix well. Pour the warm stock over the couscous and then cover the bowl with a lid or plate for 10 minutes to allow the couscous to absorb the stock without losing heat.

Meanwhile, heat a frying pan and dry-fry the flaked almonds for 1–2 minutes or until they are golden brown, to give them an extra crunch. Take the lid off the couscous and make sure that all of the stock has been soaked up, then add the spring onions, tomatoes, parsley, the dry-roasted flaked almonds, raisins, mint and coriander. Mix through, using a fork. Season with salt and pepper, and serve.

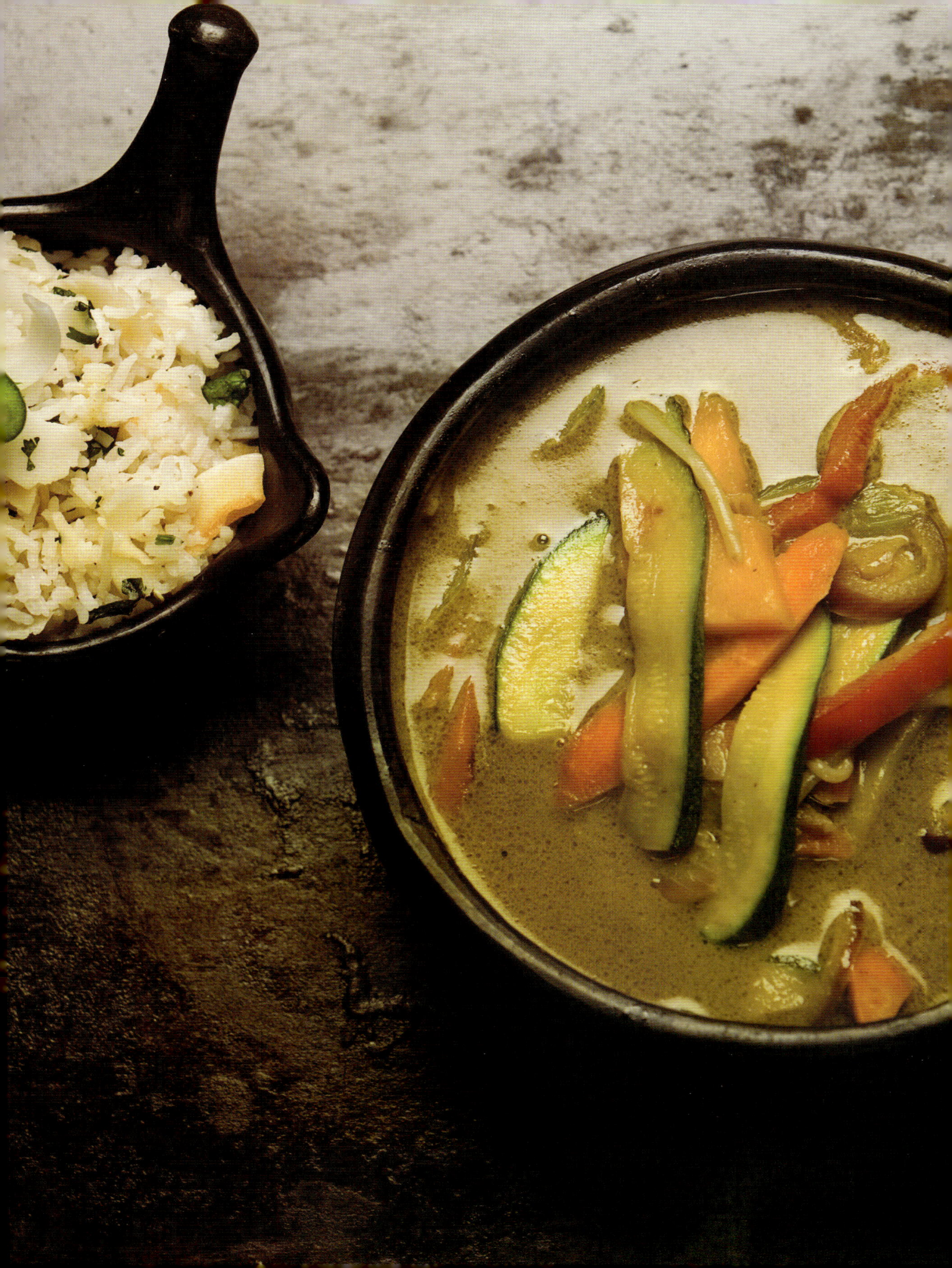

Thai green curry with coconut rice

V, GF

Don't be put off by the long list of ingredients here. The recipe is actually really simple; we make this at home as a quick dinner because the kids love it, and if you are in a rush just make plain jasmine rice. We cook our rice in a rice cooker and it is ready at the same time as the curry.

Serves 8

4 tbsp vegetable oil
4 medium onions, peeled and diced
3 cloves of garlic, finely diced
3 x 400ml cans of coconut milk
60g brown sugar
2 tsp tamari
2 tbsp vegetable oil
100g shitake mushrooms
half a large aubergine or 3 baby aubergines, cut into 5cm chunks
half a red onion, chopped
half a butternut squash, peeled and chopped into 3mm slices
30g bamboo shoots
half a courgette, sliced lengthways
1 medium bunch of coriander, leaves chopped
30g bean sprouts

For the paste:
6 sticks of lemon grass
30g galangal, peeled and roughly chopped
50g ginger, peeled and roughly chopped
6 small shallots, peeled and cut in half
2 medium green chillies, deseeded and roughly chopped
2 large bunches of coriander, finely chopped (use the stalks as well)
4 cloves of garlic, chopped
4 tbsp of concentrated liquid tamarind
200ml vegetable oil
2 tbsp ground ginger
4 tbsp ground cumin
10 fresh lime leaves

Make the paste first. Cut the dry ends off the lemon grass, remove the outer layers and roughly chop the soft inner leaves, then blend all the paste ingredients in a food processor (if you are unable to get galangal, just increase the ginger to 80g). Set it to one side.

Heat the vegetable oil in a large pan. Add the onions and gently brown them for 3 minutes, then add the garlic and cook for another 2 minutes. Lower the heat and add the curry paste to the onions and garlic. Cook for another 10 minutes, stirring continuously; you may need to add a little water if this curry sauce starts to thicken. At this point all the ingredients should start to release a bouquet of lovely aromas. Add the coconut milk, turn up the heat and bring it to the boil. Add the brown sugar and salt to taste, then lower to a gentle heat and simmer for 30 minutes.

Put a colander or fine sieve over a large bowl, and carefully sieve the curry sauce into it. Add the tamari to the sauce and stir it in.

Put a wok over a high heat. When it is hot, add 2 tablespoons of vegetable oil, then put in the mushrooms and cook them for a couple of minutes. Then add the aubergine. After 2–3 minutes add the red onion and cook for a further 2–3 minutes. Add the butternut and bamboo shoots and stir-fry everything together for 1-2 minutes (if you wish, you could add some green chopped chilli at this point).

Add the curry sauce to the wok, cover it and bring to the boil. Lower the heat and simmer for 5–10 minutes until the vegetables are cooked but not too soft – you want to keep as much of the crunch as possible.

When you are almost ready, add the courgettes and cook them for 2 minutes. Then stir in some chopped coriander and bean sprouts and serve with coconut rice.

Coconut rice

a little vegetable oil
400g jasmine rice
400ml tin of good coconut milk
2 tbsp dry shredded coconut, unsweetened
½ tsp salt
½ large green chilli (optional garnish)

Oil the bottom of a large saucepan using kitchen paper. Pour the rice, coconut milk and ½ can of water (use a coconut milk can as a measure) into the pan. Add the shredded coconut and the salt, stir the pan, and put it on a high heat. Stir continuously so that the rice does not stick to the bottom.

As soon as it begins to boil, stop stirring. Place a tight fitting lid on top of the pan and turn the heat to the lowest setting.

Allow the rice to simmer for 15 minutes until all the liquid has been absorbed. As soon as there is no liquid left, turn off the heat – but leave the pot on the hob for another 5–10 minutes with the lid on so that the rice continues to steam. Check that it is not sticking. When you are ready to serve, use a fork to fluff the rice up, check for seasoning and scatter with diagonally sliced chilli if using.

GF
Baby carrot and mushroom stroganoff with brown basmati and wild rice

This is real comfort food which does not take very long to prepare; it's great when it's cold outside and you want something to warm you up. The beauty of using the brown rice with the wild rice is that they take the same time to cook, unlike white rice which cooks more quickly.

Serves 8

- 1kg mixed mushrooms, e.g. oyster, portobello, chestnut
- 250g butter
- 3 tbsp vegetable oil
- 2 medium onions, finely chopped
- 8 cloves of garlic, finely chopped
- 1 large bunch of parsley, finely chopped
- 200g fresh tarragon or fresh thyme (remove leaves from stalks and chop finely)
- 150ml brandy
- 100ml strong vegetable stock
- 200g baby carrots, washed, stalks removed and cut in half lengthways
- 1 litre crème fraiche
- 1 tsp white wine vinegar
- salt and pepper

For the rice:
- 400g brown basmati rice
- 125g wild rice
- 1tsp salt
- 1.2l water

Start the rice first. Place the water and salt in a large pan and bring to the boil, add the two types of rice and gently cook them on a low heat for 25 minutes. When you add the rice, stir it with a spoon to stop it sticking to the bottom of the pan, but do not touch the rice after that until it is ready.

Chop the mushrooms into pieces that are approximately 5cm in size. Melt the butter with the oil in another large pan and sweat the onions. Add the garlic after 5 minutes. Add the chopped mushrooms, along with the parsley and tarragon or thyme. Cook for 10 minutes until everything is soft, then add the brandy and vegetable stock. Give the pan a good stir to allow the mushrooms to absorb the liquids. Add the baby carrot halves.

Then add the crème fraiche and mix it in well. Cook gently for another 10 minutes, by which time the sauce will have turned slightly brown. Take the pan off the heat, stir in the wine vinegar and season to taste with a good grinding of fresh black pepper and a little salt if needed. Accompany with the rice and your favourite greens.

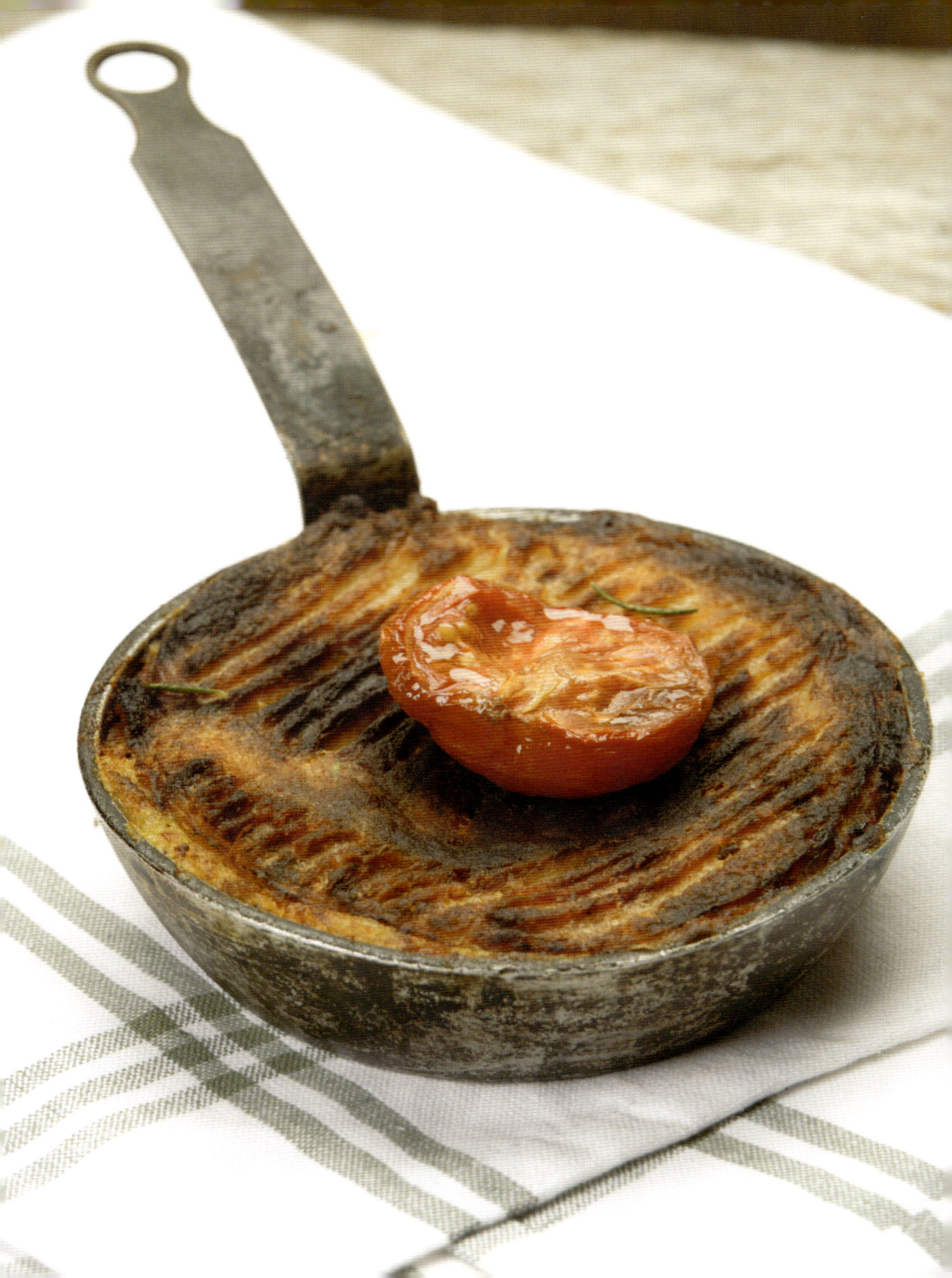

VO, GF
Cassava and puy lentil shepherdess pie

This dish is a family favourite and a great comfort food which can be used in different ways. Instead of making up into a pie you could just serve the stew on top of slow-cooked crispy jacket potatoes with a knob of butter and a sprinkling of sea salt.

Serves 6–8

1 tbsp olive oil
1 medium onion, finely chopped
6 cloves of garlic, finely chopped
1 tbsp ground cumin
1½ tsp turmeric
1 tsp ground cinnamon
350g Puy lentils
2 x 400g tins of chopped tomatoes
650ml cold water
1 tbsp salt
600g cassava squash, peeled and chopped into 1cm cubes
300g petit pois

For the mashed-potato topping:
1kg potatoes
50g butter or vegan margarine
1tbsp milk or soya milk
salt and pepper

Heat the oil in a large saucepan and add the onion. When it is soft add the garlic and cook for a minute before adding the spices, stirring all the time. Add the lentils and stir them through, then add the tinned tomatoes and cover the pan. Allow them to cook for 4–5 minutes.

Then add the water and salt, and cook for a further 15 minutes, keeping the lid on, by which time the lentils should be about half cooked. Add the cassava and, if needed, another 5 tablespoons or so of water. Cover and cook for a further 40 minutes.

Take the lid off the pan and check that the lentils are cooked and the seasoning is right. Add the petit pois and cook for another minute, then take the pan off the heat. At this stage you can use the lentil stew as you wish.

To continue with the shepherdess pie, preheat the oven to 180°C/gas mark 4. Peel 1kg of potatoes and cut them into chunks, put them in a pan of cold water and bring it to the boil. Cook for 25 minutes until the potatoes are nice and soft. Add vegan margarine (or butter) and a drop of soya milk (or ordinary milk) and season with salt and pepper. Mash the potatoes by hand or put them through a potato ricer. Pour the lentil stew into a large casserole dish, top it with the potato and bake it in the oven for 25 minutes until nice and golden brown on top.

Feta, butternut squash, caramelised onion and cashew-nut wellington, page 132

Special occasions

Food for Friends Sunday roast

We normally serve these on Sundays with all the roast trimmings and gravy. However you could also serve them with the potato gratin dauphinois (opposite) and steamed seasonal vegetables.

Makes 12 escalopes

500g Puy lentils
250g chestnuts, peeled
half a bunch of spring onions
1 small bunch of parsley
half a bunch of celery
300g vegetarian blue cheese (such as dolcelatte)
2 large eggs, beaten
325g breadcrumbs
200g vegetarian pecorino or other hard cheese, grated
3 eggs
4 tbsp flour
vegetable oil for frying

Put the lentils into a large pan of cold water and bring it to the boil. Reduce the heat to a steady simmer and cook for about 1 hour or until they are soft but not mushy. Drain them and refresh under running water.

Preheat the oven to 180°C/gas mark 4. Dice the chestnuts, finely chop the spring onions, parsley and celery and place them in a large bowl. Add the cooked lentils and crumble in the blue cheese. Then add the beaten eggs, 200g of the breadcrumbs and the grated pecorino. Using your hands, mix together for a good 10 minutes, by which time you should have a solid paste with which to make the escalopes. Because the cheeses are salty you shouldn't need to add salt but at this point taste the mixture and adjust the seasoning if necessary.

Break the three eggs into a bowl and whisk them. Put the flour in another and the remaining breadcrumbs in a third, and have a baking sheet ready for the finished escalopes. Form the escalopes by making a ball of lentil mixture about the size of a lime in your hands, and then flatten it out so it is about 1.5cm thick. Dust it in the flour bowl (shake off the excess), then dip it in the egg wash and then in the breadcrumbs; don't forget to do both sides. Put it to one side and repeat until all are done.

Use a frying pan with a little vegetable oil, and fry each one very quickly on both sides for 30 seconds. Put them on the baking sheet and cook in the oven for 10–15 minutes or until crisp and cooked through.

GF
Potato gratin dauphinois

This is an old favourite side dish, especially for big festive feasts, Sunday roasts or even buffets. You can prepare it in advance and keep it in the fridge until you're ready to bake it.

Serves 4

- 1kg désirée potatoes
- 500ml milk
- 1 bouquet garni
- freshly grated nutmeg
- salt and white pepper
- 1 clove of garlic, halved
- 25g butter, softened
- 150ml double cream
- 100g vegetarian gruyère cheese, grated

Preheat the oven to 200°C/gas mark 6. Peel the potatoes and slice them thinly. Bring the milk to a boil in a large pan. Add the bouquet garni and nutmeg, and salt and pepper to taste. Carefully put the potatoes in the pan and return it to the boil. Lower the heat and allow to simmer for 10–15 minutes. Then drain the potatoes but reserve the milk.

Rub the halved garlic over the inside of a 22cm x 33cm baking dish. Butter the dish well, and layer the potatoes in it, seasoning each layer.

Put the milk back in the pan. Add the cream to the milk and bring it almost to a boil. Remove it from the heat and pour the creamy milk over the potatoes. Top with the grated cheese and bake for about 40 minutes.

VO
Food for Friends red wine and date gravy

This recipe can be used with our sausage recipes or any of the Special Occasions dishes, such as the wellington or escalopes. Make sure you use vegan wine for the vegan option.

Serves 4

- 1 tbsp vegetable oil
- 3 medium onions, finely sliced
- 3 cloves of garlic, finely chopped
- 400ml red wine
- 2tsp chopped rosemary
- 80g dried dates
- 2tsp marmite

Heat the oil in a pan and sweat the onions until they are golden brown. Add the garlic and cook for a further 3 minutes. Add the wine and the chopped herbs and bring to the boil.

Put the dates in a food processor and add a large ladle of hot liquid along with the marmite. Blend to a smooth paste. Return to the saucepan and reduce the heat to low. Cook for a further 10 minutes before serving.

VO, N

Feta, butternut squash, caramelised onion and cashew-nut wellingtons

These are a lovely alternative to a Sunday roast or traditional festive meal with all the trimmings, but just like the Food for Friends escalopes on page 130 they are also great as a simple dinner with vegetables or salad.

Serves 8

2tbsp butter or vegan margarine
2 large white onions, finely chopped
20g caster sugar
1.2kg butternut squash, peeled and deseeded
2 tbsp olive oil
50g cashew nuts
salt and pepper
1 medium bunch of chives, finely chopped
100g feta, crumbled
4 vegan filo pastry sheets approx 30cm x 24cm
100g fresh baby spinach, washed
a little vegan margarine, melted
a few poppy seeds

Preheat the oven to 180°C/gas mark 4. Melt the butter in a pan and fry the onions over a medium heat for approximately 10 minutes, until they are golden brown. Add the sugar, stir through and cook for a further 10 minutes.

Dice the butternut squash into small pieces, put them on a baking tray and drizzle with the olive oil. Roast them in the oven for 30 minutes or until they are soft. Place in a bowl and allow to cool.

Spread the cashew nuts out on another baking tray and roast in the oven for 5 minutes. Take them out, give the tray a good shake and then put them back for another 5 minutes, until golden.

Mash the roasted butternut squash and season with salt and pepper. Add the finely chopped chives, caramelised onions and feta and mix them together well.

Unwrap the filo pastry and lie it flat, covering it with a damp tea towel to stop it from drying out. Take two pieces of filo and put one on top of the other. Spoon half the mixture into the middle and make a long shape; leave a 5cm edge of pastry around the edges. Place half the spinach leaves on top of the mixture and then half the roasted cashew nuts. Brush the edges of the pastry with the melted margarine. Then roll up the pastry, tucking the short sides in as you roll to keep it neat, and making sure the seam ends up underneath. The end result should be a neat oblong parcel with tucked-in sides.

Brush the top with some more melted margarine and sprinkle with poppy seeds, Carefully put the parcel on a large baking sheet. Repeat the same procedure with the remaining ingredients to make a second wellington. Bake them in the oven for 25 minutes until golden brown.

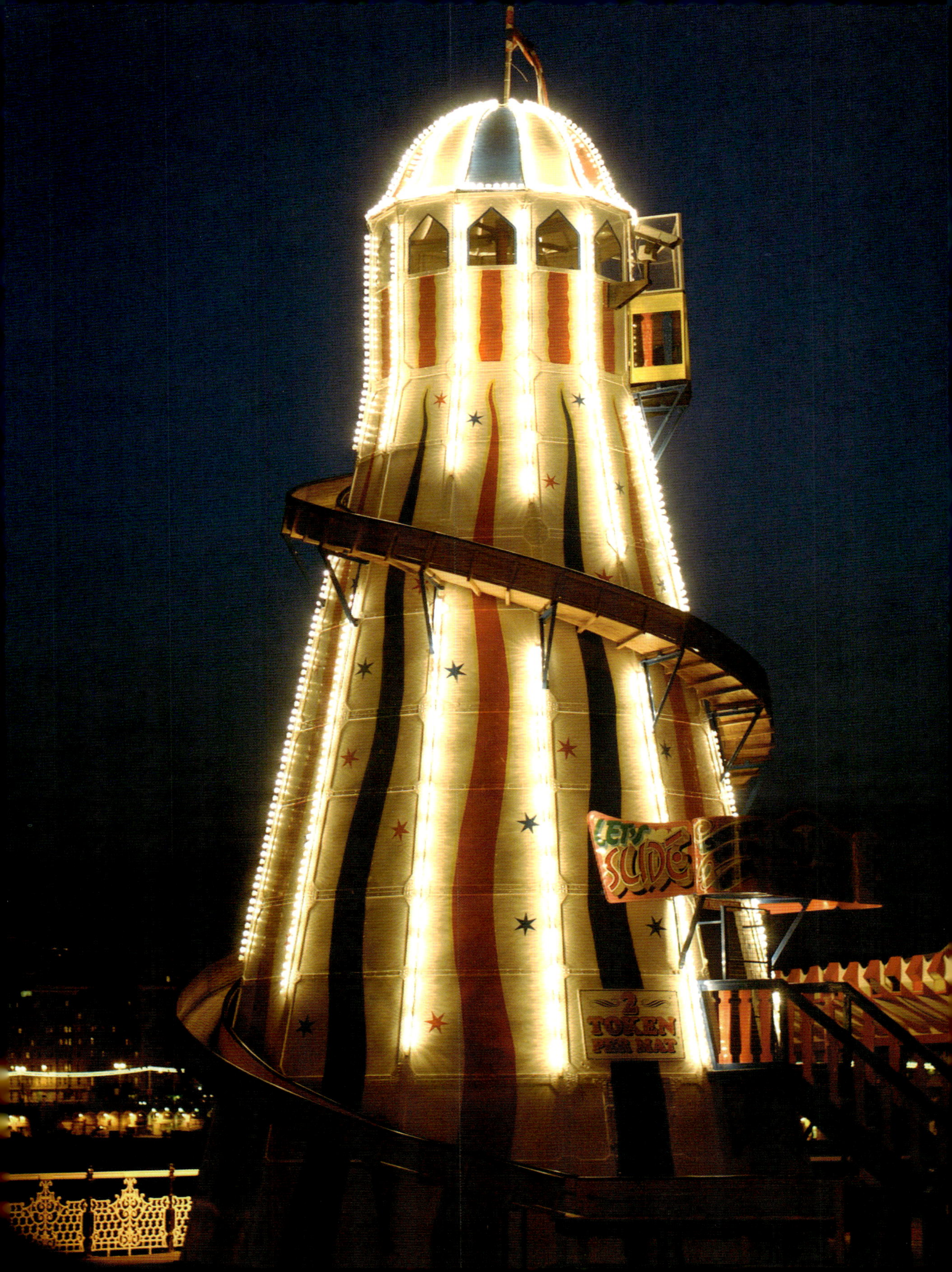
LET'S
SLIDE
2
TOKEN
PER MAT

GF, N
Food for Friends gluten-free Christmas pudding

Our gluten-free Christmas pud can easily be suitable for people with nut allergies too; just leave out the almonds. This recipe makes two puddings – you will need two 1.2 litre pudding basins – and they store well in a dry place for up to three months.

Each pudding serves 6

250g raisins
225g sultanas
450g currants
85g mixed peel
finely grated juice and zest of 1 orange, plus the juice of another
finely grated zest and juice of 1 lemon
1 tsp mixed spice
½ tsp ground cinnamon
½ tsp grated nutmeg
150ml Earl Grey tea, cold
6 tbsp brandy or rum
1 large cooking apple, peeled, cored and grated
85g blanched almonds, chopped
350g dark brown sugar
2 tbsp black treacle
225g vegetarian suet
225g gluten-free breadcrumbs
50g rice flour
50g cornflour
2 tsp baking powder
1 tsp salt
5 large eggs, beaten
a little butter

Put the dried fruit, mixed peel, citrus zest and juices, spices, cold tea and the brandy or rum in a large bowl. Mix everything together and leave it to soak overnight. The next day, mix in the apple, almonds, brown sugar and treacle.

Using another large bowl, mix the suet, breadcrumbs, rice flour, cornflour, baking powder and salt together, then gradually beat in the eggs until smooth. Stir in the soaked fruit.

Grease two 1.2 litre pudding basins with the vegan margarine, and divide the mixture between the basins until they are both about two-thirds full. Cover the top of each pudding with a circle of baking paper. Then fold a 2cm pleat across the middle of two large pieces of foil and use a piece to cover the top of each basin; the foil should overhang. Secure it with string. Place upturned sauces into two deep saucepans, sit a pudding basin on top of each saucer and fill the saucepans with boiling water to come half-way up the basins. Cover and steam for 8 hours, topping up the boiling water when the levels drop.

Remove the bowls from the pans. Carefully turn them out, and serve. If you want to store the puddings, allow them to cool down in the bowl. Then cover with fresh baking paper and foil, and finally add a layer of cling film. Keep them in a dry place. To reheat, steam for 2 hours or microwave on medium for 6–7 minutes, and serve.

GF, N
Mince pies

To allow the flavour to develop fully, the mincemeat should be made at least a month in advance of being used; it is very easy, very delicious and this recipe makes about 1.125kg. If you need your mince pies to be nut free as well as gluten free, just leave the almonds out of the mincemeat.

Makes 12

For the pastry:
100g rice flour, plus extra for dusting
100g fine yellow cornmeal
½ tsp salt
100g chilled butter, diced
1 medium free-range egg, beaten

For the mincemeat:
100g sultanas
175g raisins
175g currants
175g grated Bramley apples
100g vegetarian suet
200g soft brown sugar
100g finely chopped mixed peel
75g blanched and chopped almonds
½ tbsp mixed spice
zest and juice of one orange
a large splash of brandy

To make the mincemeat, mix all the ingredients together in a large bowl and then spoon into some sterile jars (for more on sterilising jars, see page 10) and seal. It will keep for 12 months.

Prepare the pastry for the mince pies. Sift the flour, cornmeal and salt into a large mixing bowl. Add the butter and rub it into the flour with your fingertips until the mixture resembles fine breadcrumbs.

Using a table knife, stir in the egg until the mixture clumps together. Bring the dough together into a ball. Knead it lightly on a work surface dusted with rice flour, until smooth. Wrap in cling film and chill in the fridge for at least 30 minutes to firm up – this will make it easier to roll. Preheat the oven to 200°C/gas mark 6. Put a large piece of cling film on the worktop and flour it well. Put the pastry on the cling film and put another piece, also floured, on top – this will help hold the pastry together. Roll out the pastry between the two pieces of cling film.

Peel the cling film away from both sides carefully before using a 7–8cm cutter to cut out 24 pastry rounds. Use 12 rounds to line a 12-hole mince pie tin. Fill with mincemeat and top with the rest of the pastry rounds. Make two holes at the top of each mince pie to allow the steam to escape and put the tin in the oven. Bake for 15–20 minutes. Cool them on a wire rack and then dust with icing sugar before serving.

Pear and tofu chocolate torte, page 140

Desserts

Tiramisu profiteroles with chocolate sauce

This recipe needs some time, but you can make the profiteroles in advance and they will keep in an air-tight container, or you could even freeze them.

Serves 6–8 (makes about 25 and allows for sample tastings!)

For the profiteroles' choux pastry:
375g unsalted butter, chopped into cubes
875ml cold water (this measure must be exact)
425g plain flour
11 eggs

For the tiramisu mousse:
100ml Kahlua or Tia Maria
2 shots of espresso
500g caster sugar
500ml double cream
500ml mascarpone

For the chocolate sauce:
100ml double cream
400g dark chocolate (min. 70% cocoa solids)

Make the profiteroles first. In a deep saucepan, bring the butter and cold water to the boil. Have the flour ready and as soon as the butter has melted and the water is beginning to boil and foam, turn the heat to low (or move the pan to a very low ring if you are using an electric hob). Immediately add all the flour, stir and beat furiously with a spoon until the mix comes away from the edges of the pan. Turn it out of the pan into a cold bowl and allow it to cool for 20–30 minutes.

Preheat the oven to 180°C/gas mark 4. Then, using a hand whisk or a mixer on a low speed, add the eggs one at a time until all have been amalgamated – do not over-beat the mixture.

Cover a baking tray with baking paper. Take a piping bag with a 2cm plain nozzle, fill it with the pastry dough and pipe golf-ball-sized spheres onto the baking paper. Put the tray in the oven and bake the profiteroles for 20 minutes or until firm and golden. Remove them from the oven and pierce a hole in the bottom of each one. Put them back on the tray and return them to the oven for further 5 minutes until the insides have dried out, then take them out and allow them to cool. When they have cooled they can be filled or frozen.

Make the tiramisu mousse for filling the profiteroles. Put the Kahlua, espresso shots and sugar in a pan and bring to the boil. Allow the alcohol to burn off and the liquid to reduce for 5 minutes, then put the pan in a cool place for 10 minutes.

Whisk the double cream in a bowl until it thickens, but not as much as clotted cream does. Stir in the mascarpone. When the Kahlua and espresso mixture has cooled, stir it into the cream mix and keep it in the fridge until needed.

Prepare the chocolate sauce. Put a glass bowl over a pan of simmering water and make sure that the bottom of the glass bowl does not touch the water. Put the double cream and chocolate in the bowl and whisk them together until the sauce is glossy. Keep it warm while you fill the profiteroles.

Using a small piping bag, pipe the tiramisu mousse into the hole at the bottom of the profiteroles. Arrange the profiteroles on the serving dish, and then pour the warm chocolate sauce over them.

V, N
Pear and tofu chocolate torte

Over the last five years we have had more requests from our customers for this recipe than any other dish. It is loved by vegans, vegetarians and carnivores alike.

Serves 8

- 70g dark chocolate (min. 70% cocoa solids)
- 1 large pear, cored and peeled
- 1 packet (350g) firm silken tofu
- 50g caster sugar
- 60g ground almonds
- 100g golden syrup
- 10g vegan margarine
- 10 vegan biscuits, crushed

Preheat the oven to 160°C/gas mark 2–3.

Melt the chocolate in a bowl over a pan of simmering water and keep it warm.

Blend the pear and silken tofu together in a food processor. Then add the sugar, almonds and golden syrup. Make sure they are blended together well. While the food processor is running, pour the chocolate in. Continue processing until everything is completely blended.

Melt the vegan margarine and mix it thoroughly with the crushed biscuits. Put a layer at the bottom of a sprung-bottom 25cm cake tin and press it down firmly. Pour the pear, tofu and chocolate mix onto the base and smooth the top. Put the tin in the oven and bake for 30–45 minutes, until the top does not stick to the fingers when touched. Put it to one side to cool down, then refrigerate until set. Serve with fresh berries, a berry compote or soya cream.

GF
Turkish Delight parfait with a rosewater coulis

This dessert is great on a hot summer's day as it is fragrant and light – it looks so pretty when served with the coulis and a scattering of rose petals. You can easily make this dessert in advance, as it will keep well for a month in the freezer. The coulis can be bottled and also makes a lovely chilled summer drink – put two tablespoons in a tall glass, add crushed ice and top up with still or sparkling water.

Serves 8

400ml double cream
2 standard packets of Fry's Turkish Delight or, if unavailable, 100g milk chocolate-covered turkish delight, chopped
2 tsp rosewater
5 egg whites
4 tbsp caster sugar
rose petals, to serve (optional)

For the rosewater coulis:
400g granulated sugar
250ml water
1 tbsp lemon juice
5 tbsp rosewater
a few drops of grenadine (optional, for colour)

Line a 900g loaf tin with baking paper, letting the paper overhang the edges so that it can be brought over the top to cover the parfait.

Gently heat 5 tablespoons of the double cream in a small pan. Add the chopped pieces of Turkish Delight until the chocolate and a little of the actual Turkish Delight have melted. Then add the rosewater and set it aside to cool slightly.

In a mixer, or using an electric whisk and a large bowl, whip the egg whites into soft peaks. Then slowly add the sugar and continue whisking for another minute.

In another bowl, whisk the rest of the double cream into soft peaks. Then carefully fold the cream into the egg mixture, and add the Turkish Delight and cream, still stirring gently. Pour it into the bread tin, gently fold over the overlapping baking paper and put the tin in the freezer for a minimum of 4 hours.

Make the rosewater coulis. Put the sugar and water into a pan (don't use an aluminium one) and heat them gently, stirring from time to time, until the sugar is completely dissolved. Add the lemon juice and simmer for 10 minutes without stirring; skim off any froth that rises. Add the rosewater and grenadine, if you are using it. Stir and simmer for a further 2 minutes, then remove the pan from the heat and allow the mixture to cool slightly. Put into sterilised bottles and seal; when it's completely cold, store it in the fridge. It will last up to three months without losing any intensity if it's stored in a sterilised and sealed bottle.

Serve slices of parfait with a drizzle of rosewater coulis and a scattering of rose petals.

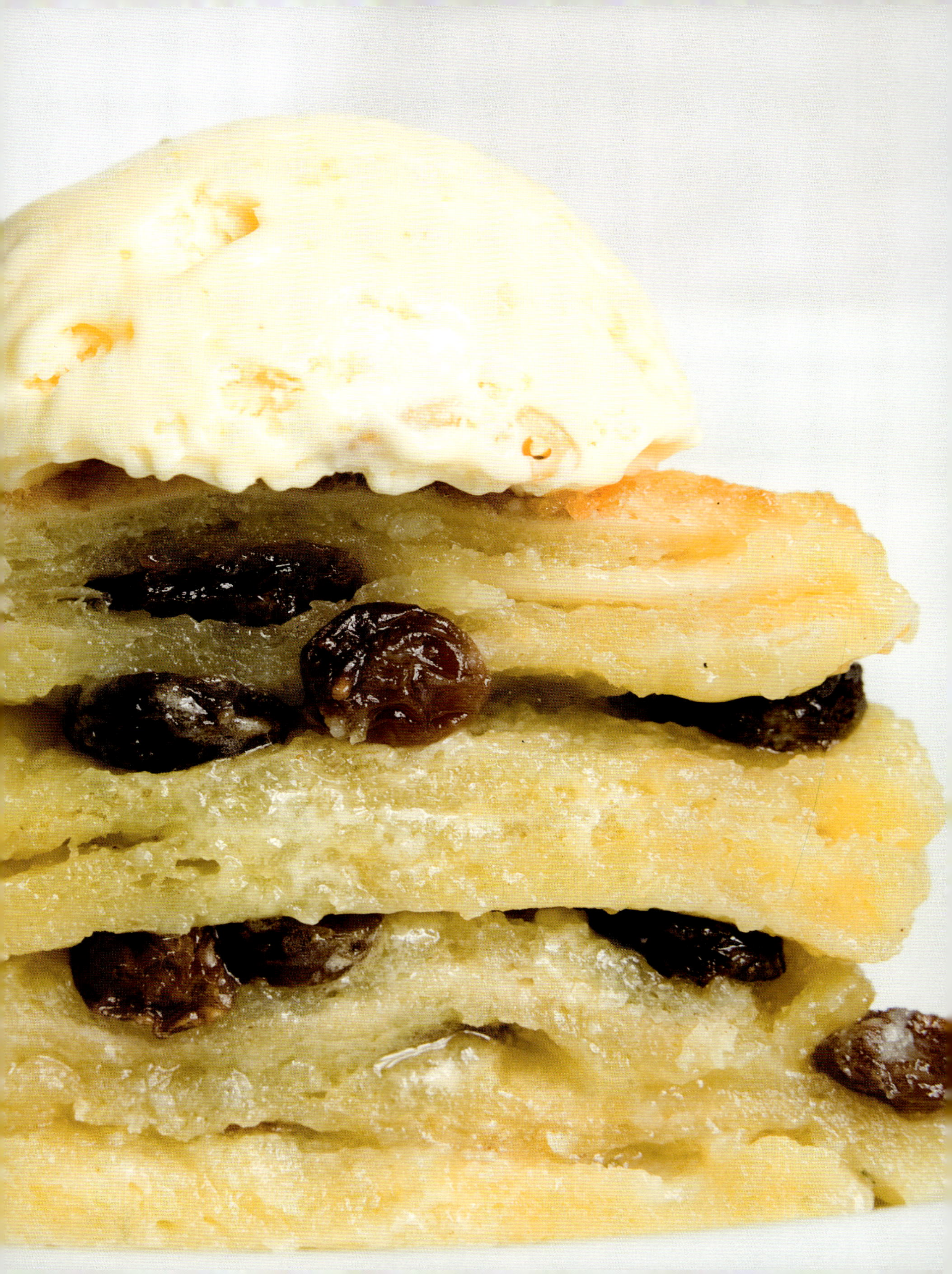

White chocolate bread and butter puddings

Serves 8

a little butter
4 eggs
200ml milk
200ml double cream
100g honey
a standard 800g loaf of thickly sliced white bread
a handful of sultanas, or a few dried apricots, chopped
100g white chocolate, in medium chunks, or large white chocolate buttons
a little brown sugar, for sprinkling

Preheat the oven to 180°C/gas mark 4. Grease 8 x 150ml ramekins with butter and then line the bases with a circle of baking paper.

Mix the eggs, milk, cream and honey together in a bowl and set it aside.

Using a circular cutter, approximately 8cm diameter, cut out 24 circles of bread for the base, middle and top of each pudding. Then cut strips of bread (no crusts) to fit around the sides of the ramekins. Place one circle of bread in the bottom of each ramekin, then tightly fit the strips of bread vertically around the sides; don't worry if they aren't completely straight at the top, as this will become the bottom when you turn the puddings out of the ramekins.

Then put 4 or 5 sultanas (or a few pieces of apricot) and three buttons or two chunks of white chocolate in the bottom of each ramekin. Put another circle of bread over them. Ladle some of the milk and cream mixture over each of the puddings and then soak the final bread circles in the mixture before placing them on top of each ramekin. Ladle a little more milk and cream mixture over the top of each pudding and then sprinkle a little brown sugar over them.

Put the ramekins in a deep oven tray or baking dish. Fill the tray with hot water until it comes half way up the sides of the ramekins. Cook the puddings in the oven for 20 minutes or until they are golden brown. Serve them immediately with homemade vanilla ice cream, or our Baileys ice cream (see page 147).

GF
Saffron and cardamom crème caramel

Makes 4

250g granulated sugar
225 ml water
4 eggs, beaten
100g caster sugar
600ml full-fat milk
1 cardamom pod, crushed
half a vanilla pod, split
1 tsp vanilla essence
a pinch of saffron

Preheat the oven to 170°C/gas mark 3, and put some cold water and ice into a container large enough to take the base of a saucepan.

Make the caramel. Put the granulated sugar and water into a clean heavy saucepan – a really clean one is important as anything in the pan can turn the caramel into a sugar syrup. Gently bring it to the boil, then lower the heat and gently swirl the pan once or twice, but do not stir it at all. When the syrup changes into a light brown colour, remove the pan from the heat and plunge the base of the pan into the iced water to prevent further cooking. Then remove the pan to stop the caramel setting. Immediately pour the hot caramel into 4 x 150ml ramekins, swirling to coat the bottom and sides. If the caramel hardens as you are pouring it, reheat it very gently.

Now make the saffron and cardamom custard. Mix the eggs and caster sugar together gently, to avoid them foaming up.

Put the milk in a pan and add the cardamom, vanilla pod and vanilla essence. Warm over a gentle heat, and remove the pan from the heat when the milk is hand hot. Gradually add the milk to the egg and sugar mix. Add the saffron and then strain the mixture into a jug. Leave it to settle.

Put the ramekins in a deep oven tray or baking dish and fill it with warm water to come half way up the side of the ramekins. Then gently pour the custard mixture into ramekins, filling them to the brim, and bake them in the oven for 30–40 minutes. They should wobble slightly when ready, but not ripple like water. Allow them to cool down, and then chill them in the fridge.

To serve the crèmes caramels gently loosen the edges of the custard and turn each out upside down on to a plate, so that the caramel runs around the plate.

Cranberry crèmes brûlées

GF

This is good for entertaining, because both the compôte and the brûlées can be made up to two days in advance and kept chilled.

Makes 6

For the cranberry compôte:
250g cranberries, fresh or frozen
a few broad strips of pared orange zest, plus extra zest for serving
50g caster sugar

For the custard:
6 medium egg yolks
3 heaped tbsp caster sugar
1 vanilla pod, split lengthways, seeds removed and pod discarded
600ml double cream
icing sugar for dusting

For the caramel:
125g caster sugar

Preheat the oven to 160°C/gas mark 2–3. You will also need to have 6 x 150ml ramekins ready.

To make the compôte, put the cranberries in a small saucepan with the orange zest over a low heat, and gently cook them for 5–8 minutes. Then add the sugar and heat for a few minutes more, stirring occasionally, until the sugar has melted and blended into a syrup with the juice. Transfer it into a bowl, remove the orange zest and leave it to cool.

Whisk all the ingredients for the custard, except the icing sugar, in a blender. Pass it through a sieve into a bowl. Divide half the compôte between the ramekins, and then pour the custard mixture into the ramekins on top of the compôte.

Put the ramekins in a deep oven tray or baking dish and fill it with warm water to come two-thirds of the way up the side of the ramekins. Bake for about 1 hour or until the custard is lightly golden and set; it should wobble but there should be no liquid. Take the ramekins out of the tin and allow them to cool down to room temperature.

Make the caramel. Gently heat the sugar for the caramel in a small pan until half of it has liquefied and started to colour, then stir it. Stir it constantly until it has gone a deep golden colour, then remove the pan from the heat.

Dust the top of the ramekins with icing sugar and then drizzle a teaspoon of the caramel on top; it should set hard within a couple of minutes. Cover the ramekins and chill them in the fridge for a couple of hours.

To serve the crèmes brûlées, top them with the remaining compote and orange zest.

GF
Chocolate molten pots, with Baileys ice cream

I don't know anybody who has tried this pudding and not liked it; the chocolate pots are light and fluffy with a melted chocolate middle that oozes out with the first spoonful. The home-made Baileys ice cream is not essential, but it can add a luxurious finishing touch to the dish and is also very simple to make. Another reason for this dish's popularity (people come to Food for Friends especially to have it) is that it is gluten-free. There is no alternative option on this as we feel it's a good dish for everyone.

Serves 4

125g dark chocolate (at least 73% cocoa solids)
125g unsalted butter
2 eggs
3 egg yolks
65g caster sugar
10g gluten-free flour

Preheat the oven to 200°C/gas mark 6, and have 4 x 150ml ramekins to hand. Put the chocolate and butter in a bowl over a saucepan of simmering water on the hob and allow them to melt; don't let the bowl touch the surface of the water. While they melt, whisk the eggs and sugar together until they are pale in colour and form soft peaks.

Sieve the flour into the mix, and then pour in the melted chocolate. Gently fold these into the mixture to combine everything. Pour the mixture into the four ramekins as soon as possible, before it begins to set.

These molten pots should be eaten straight out of the oven so keep them in the fridge until just before you are ready to cook and eat them, if you need to. When you are ready, put them in the oven. They will take 10 minutes cooling from chilled and 8 minutes from room temperature, by which time they should have risen above the top of the ramekins. If you leave them longer than this you will have a chocolate muffin!

Serve with ice cream.

Baileys ice cream

This is a very simple recipe which does not require the use of an ice-cream maker. It can also be adapted easily; instead of Baileys you could use another liqueur, or maybe add chocolate drops or even pistachios.

Makes 2 litres

7 egg whites
200g caster sugar
500ml double cream
3 tbsp Baileys liqueur

In a mixer or using a electric hand whisk, whisk the egg whites until they are fluffy. Turn the mixer or whisk onto a lower setting and slowly add the caster sugar; continue mixing. In a separate bowl, whisk the double cream to the same consistency as the egg and sugar mix. Add the whisked cream to the egg mixture and then pour in the Baileys and gently fold everything together. Pour it into a container for freezing, cover with a lid (or firmly cover with cling film or foil) and place in the freezer for 30 minutes. Then take it out, whisk it vigorously and put it back in the freezer for a minimum of 3 hours before serving.

Brazilian-style passion fruit mousse with vanilla tuiles

This recipe is very popular in Brazil, some might say it's the national dish! It's very simple to make but remember to allow chilling time overnight if possible. We serve the mousse in martini glasses with the tuile as a decoration but feel free to experiment.

Serves 6

For the mousse:
8 passion fruits
1 small can of condensed milk (397g)
475ml double cream

For the syrup:
2 passion fruits
50g caster sugar
1 ½ tsp water

For the tuiles:
3 egg whites
100g icing sugar
100g plain flour
60g unsalted butter
½ tsp vanilla extract

First make the mousse. Cut the passion fruits in half and scoop the insides into a bowl. Using a hand blender blitz up the seeds and pulp and then strain through a fine sieve. Stir this into the condensed milk.

In a second bowl, using an electric whisk, beat the cream until stiff peaks form. Gently fold a third of this into the passion fruit mixture and then add the rest of the cream. Divide into your serving dishes or glasses and chill in the fridge, ideally overnight but for a minimum of 4 hours.

To make the syrup cut the passion fruits in half and scoop the insides into a saucepan. Add the sugar and water and bring to the boil. Reduce the heat to low and allow to simmer for 10 minutes until the liquid has reduced to a syrup. Allow to cool.

Finally make the tuiles. Preheat the oven 200°C. Using a hand whisk, whisk the egg whites and icing sugar together until smooth. Stir in the flour and whisk lightly until just combined. Pour in the melted butter and vanilla extract and gently stir until smooth. Cover and allow to rest in the fridge for 30 minutes.

Place teaspoonfuls of the mixture onto a greased baking tray and spread into 5cm rounds (or shape of your choice) with a wet fork. Bake in the oven for 5–8 minutes until the edges are golden. If you would like to have curved tuiles, shape around a greased rolling pin whilst warm. Allow to cool on a wire rack.

When you are ready to serve the mousses, drizzle some syrup over the top of each one and serve the tuiles on the side or stuck into the top of each one.

Triple white and dark chocolate semifreddo with poached figs

This semifreddo can be made up to a month in advance and kept in the freezer, and the figs can be poached up to two days in advance. Keep the figs chilled but serve them at room temperature.

Serves 8

100g amaretti biscuits
3 tbsp Amaretto liqueur
500g dark chocolate, 70% cocoa solids
100g white chocolate
400ml double cream
4 large eggs, separated
100g caster sugar
seeds from 2 split vanilla pods

For the figs:
1 x 75cl bottle good wine, such as Cabernet Sauvignon
500ml ruby port
50g caster sugar
16 ripe figs

Line the base and sides of a 900g loaf tin with a large piece of cling film, ensuring there are no splits or gaps. Put it aside. Crush the amaretti biscuits in a bowl and stir in a tablespoon of the liqueur. Spoon the mixture evenly over the base of the lined tin and place it in the freezer.

Break up the dark chocolate and put it in a large bowl over a pan of simmering water; don't allow the water to reach the bottom of the bowl. Melt the chocolate, then remove it from the heat. Then place the white chocolate in another bowl and melt it in the same way.

Using an electric whisk, whip the cream to soft peaks in a bowl. Wash the whisk and, in another large bowl, beat the egg yolks with the sugar until pale and thickened.

Put the egg whites in a large clean bowl. Wash the whisk again and whisk the egg whites to stiff peaks, then gently fold them into the yolks and sugar. Mix half this mixture with the cooled and melted dark chocolate.

Divide the other half in two. Mix one part with the whipped cream, the remaining liqueur and the vanilla seeds. Mix the other with the white chocolate.

Take the tin out of the freezer. Pour the white chocolate mix in first. Lightly tap the tin on a work surface to level it, then pour in the dark chocolate mix. Tap it again and pour the liqueur and vanilla mixture on top. Gently tap the tin once more to even it out. Cover it with cling film and return it to the freezer for at least 12 hours.

Prepare the figs. Pour the wine and port into a saucepan, add the sugar and bring to a boil; let it bubble until the liquid has reduced by half. Add the figs, cover the pan and simmer over a low heat for about 10 minutes. Remove the figs and set them aside.

Return the poaching liquid to the heat and boil until it has reduced by two-thirds and formed a thick glaze. This can then also be set to one side. Warm it through before serving.

For serving, use chilled plates. Cut the semifreddo with a warmed knife, put a slice on each plate, add two figs alongside and drizzle them with the glaze.

Sticky toffee puddings with hot toffee sauce

Serves 6

100g unsalted butter at room temperature, cut into cubes
100g caster sugar
3 eggs
250g self-raising flour
400ml water
250g dates, finely chopped
1½ tsp bicarbonate of soda

For the hot toffee sauce:
200g unsalted butter
1 vanilla pod, split
400g soft dark brown sugar
250ml double cream

Preheat the oven to 180°C/gas mark 4, and butter 6 x 150ml ramekins.

Using an electric whisk or mixer, whisk the unsalted butter with the sugar until fluffy, then add the eggs one at a time and keep whisking. Carefully sieve the flour into the mixture and whisk again.

Bring the water to a boil in a saucepan, add the dates and cook for 3 minutes. Add the bicarbonate of soda. Mix well and then take the pan off the heat. Add the contents to the flour mixture and mix in well.

Ladle the mix carefully into the ramekins, but only half-fill them. Put the ramekins in a deep baking dish half-filled with warm water. Cover the dish with foil and bake in the oven for 35 minutes, or until the puddings have cooked through and risen a little.

Make the toffee sauce while they cook. Melt the butter with the split vanilla pod in a pan. Add the sugar and allow it to dissolve, then add the cream. Bring almost to the boil, and then reduce the heat and simmer gently for 15 minutes. Remove the pan from the heat and allow the sauce to cool and thicken a little.

To serve, turn the individual sticky toffee puddings out onto serving plates, drizzle them with the toffee sauce and accompany with vanilla ice-cream.

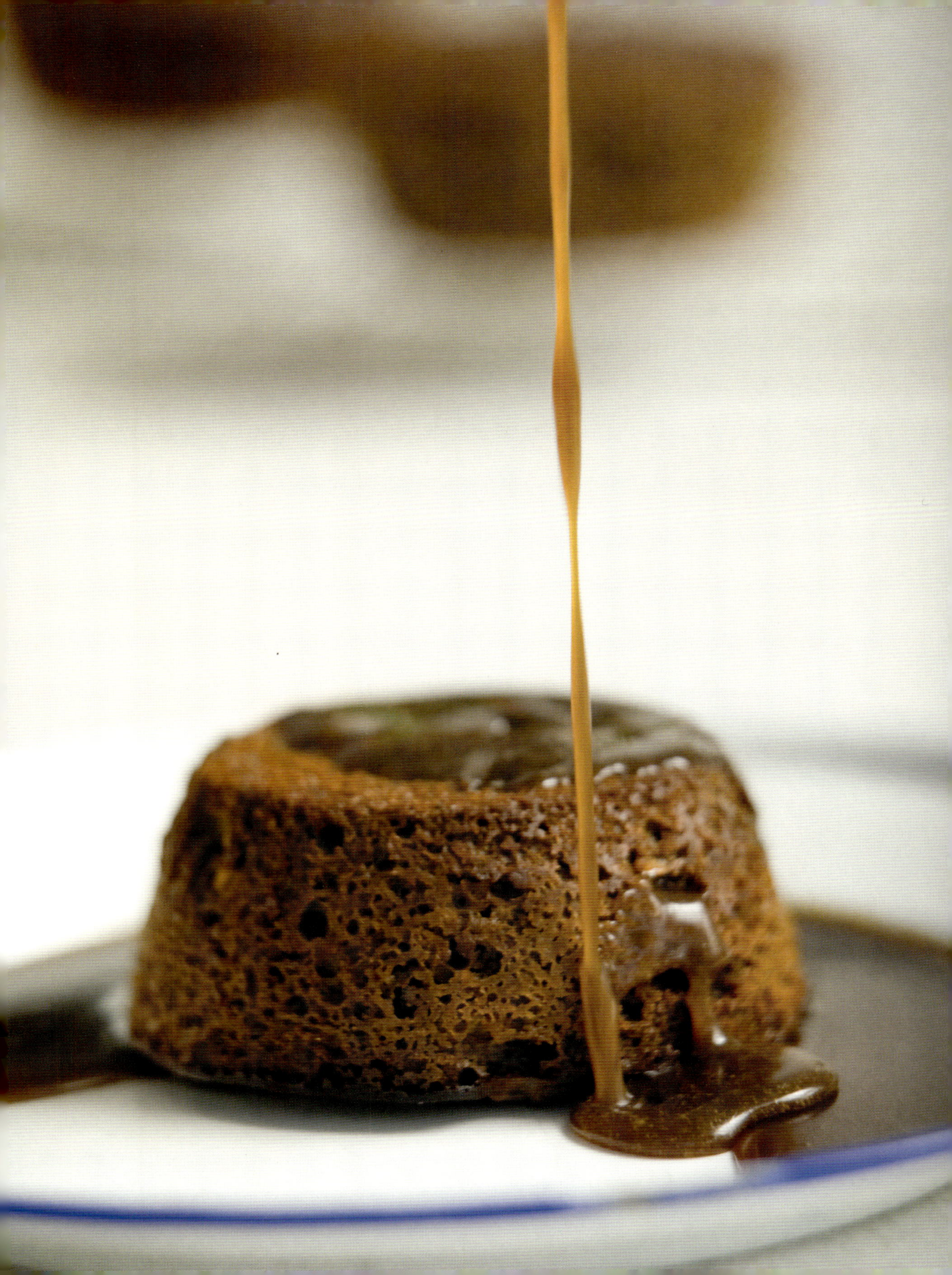

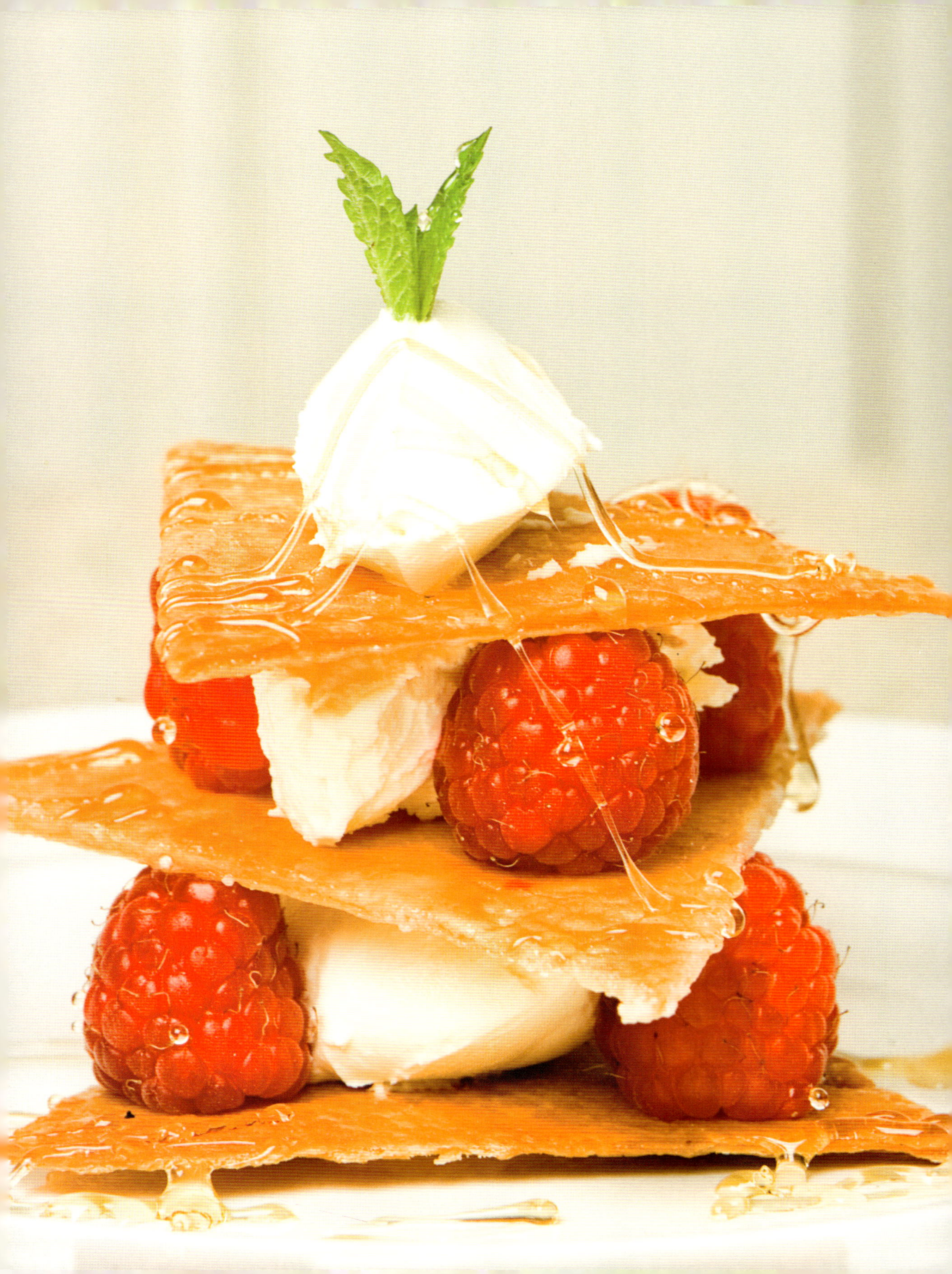

Raspberry, honey and Greek yoghurt millefeuille

This is one of those great recipes which we bring out when we need to impress some unexpected guests. It's really quick and easy, looks fab and is pretty healthy, as desserts go. You don't have to stick with raspberries; use any berries you have to hand. Blackberries are a seasonal favourite in our house. If you prefer a sugar-free dessert leave out the icing sugar.

Serves 6

a little icing sugar (optional garnish)
2 packets of ready-rolled puff pastry (30cm x 22.5cm packs)
500g Greek yoghurt
2 punnets of raspberries
some runny honey, to drizzle

Preheat the oven to 180°C/gas mark 4. Line a large baking tray with baking paper, and have another tray the same size ready.

Sprinkle a little icing sugar, if using, over a clean surface and then place the ready-rolled puff pastry on top. Roll it out a little thinner with a rolling pin.

Cut three 10cm triangles of pastry per person – 18 in total. Place the triangles on the baking paper, sprinkle with a little more icing sugar, and cover them with another piece of baking paper. Then place the other baking tray on top to stop the pastry rising. Put the trays in the oven for 7 minutes or until the pastry is cooked and crisp and golden, but not too dark. Remove from the oven and cool the pastry triangles on a wire rack.

When you are ready to serve, assemble the dessert.

Place one of the triangles on a plate, then a big dollop of yoghurt, followed by a layer of raspberries, then another pastry triangle, more yoghurt, more raspberries and then the final triangle. When you have prepared all six plates, drizzle honey over the top.

GF
Ice cream base recipe

This is a recipe to which you can add different flavours – we've suggested some – and you don't need an ice-cream machine to make it, either.

Makes 500ml

1 vanilla pod
250ml full-cream milk
300ml double cream
1 tbsp liquid glucose
4 egg yolks
100g caster sugar

Split the vanilla pod and scrape the seeds into the milk. In a large saucepan, combine the double cream, milk, glucose and the empty vanilla pod. Gently heat the milk and, just before it starts to boil, remove it from the heat and leave to infuse for 15 minutes.

Using an electric whisk, beat the eggs yolks with the sugar until smooth. Add three tablespoons of the cream mixture to the egg and sugar mix, whisking at the same time. Then pour the egg yolk mixture back into the pan of milk and warm it up gently until reaches 175°C (use a sugar thermometer). Immediately remove the pan from the heat. The mixture will have thickened at this stage, and look like a vanilla custard. Pour it into a bowl or plastic container and allow it to cool.

When it is cool, cover it and put it in the fridge for 2 hours. Then give it a good whisk, and put it in the freezer for another hour. Take it out of the freezer, whisk it again and put it back in the freezer for a minimum of 3 hours before serving.

Before you place the container in the fridge, add your chosen flavour. Try 200ml Baileys liqueur; scrape in the seeds of 4 vanilla pods; add a quick grinding of fresh black pepper, or 100g raisins soaked in 75ml dark rum, or 100g chocolate chips…

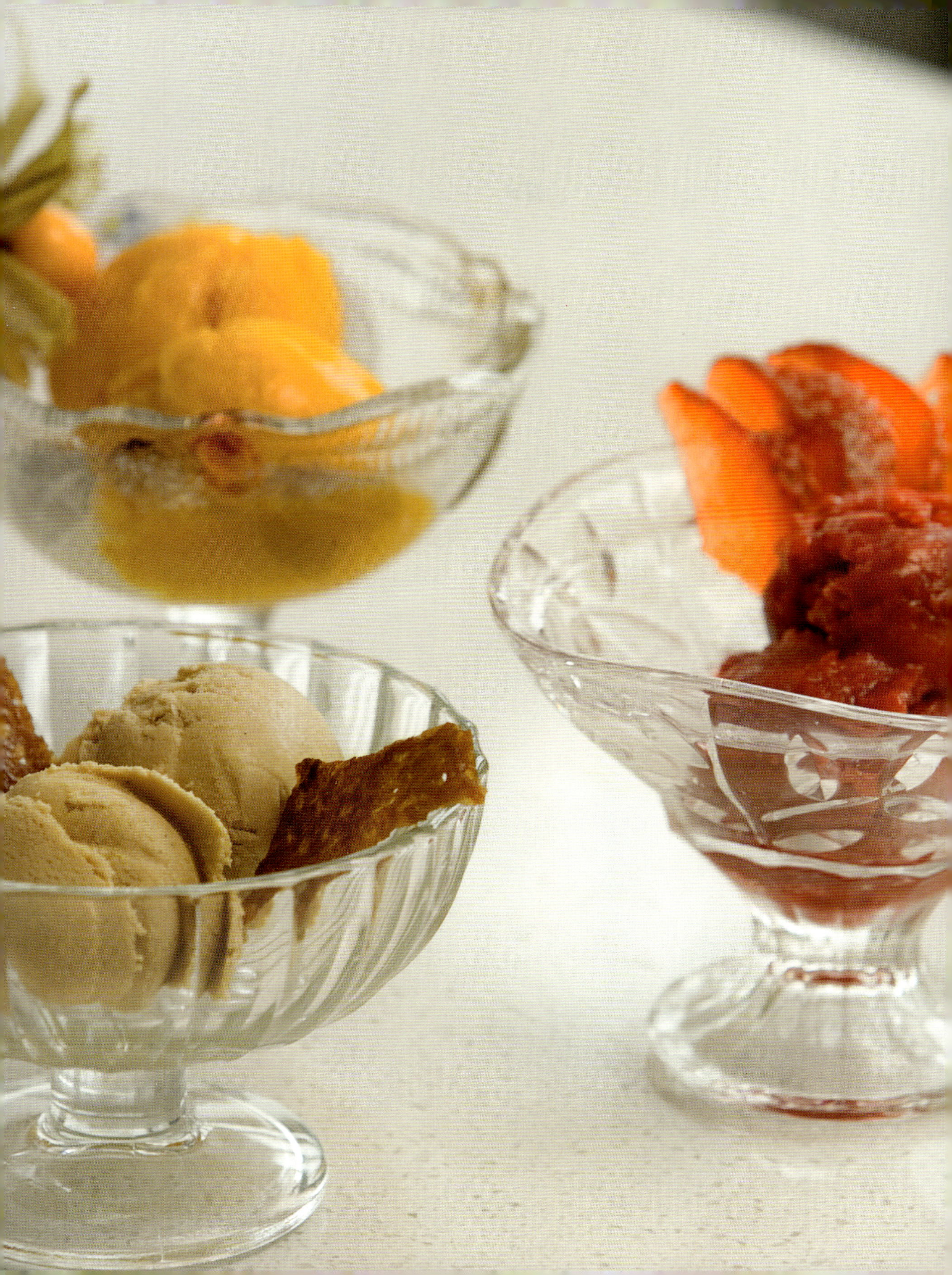

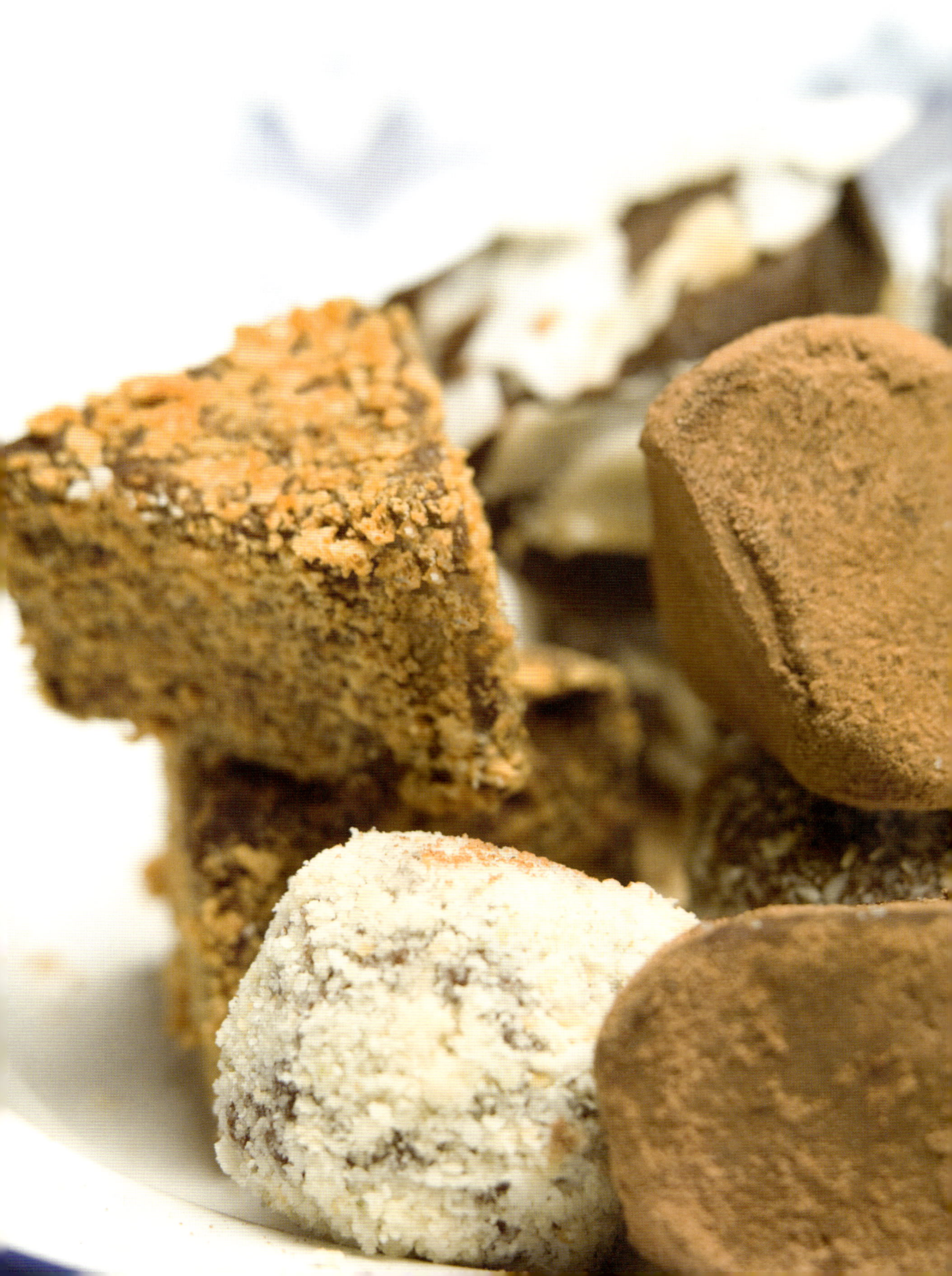

GF
Cardamom and white chocolate truffles

Try these different truffles — and there is a vegan dark chocolate alternative here, too, with other flavouring suggestions.

10 cardamom pods, crushed
425g white chocolate buttons
60g unsalted butter, room temperature, cut into small chunks
500ml whipping or double cream

Remove the seeds from the cardamom pods and crush them in a mortar and pestle. Tip the resulting spicy dust into a large bowl and add the chocolate buttons and butter.

Put the cream in a small pan and heat until just before it reaches a boil, then pour it over the cardamom and chocolate mix. Stir continuously until smooth, then whisk it until the whisk leaves a trail in the mixture (this is known as the 'ribbon stage').

Pour the mixture into a baking tray lined with baking paper, put it in the fridge and allow it to set for 3 hours.

Take the tin out of the fridge and cool your hands under the cold tap. Chop or roll the mixture into truffles using teaspoons and very cold hands. Dust the truffles with grated chocolate or icing sugar.

V
Dark chocolate truffles

450g non-dairy dark chocolate, minimum 70% solids
200ml water

Line a baking tray with cling film. Melt the chocolate with the water in a bowl over a pan full of boiling water. Fill another pan with ice. Once the chocolate has melted, remove the bowl from the heat and place it over the pan of ice. Whisk until the mixture becomes glossy and thick. Once this has occurred, scrape it out and press it into the baking tray and allow it to cool. Finish the truffles as above.

Different flavours can be added. Replace some of the water in the dark chocolate recipe with orange juice and zest, for instance. You could add almonds, rum, vanilla or white chocolate for a non-vegan version… These are best added just before the mixture becomes really thick, when beating it is still relatively easy.

Scones baking in the Food for Friends oven, page 169

Baking

GF, N
The Food for Friends gooey chocolate brownie

While there are many recipe books with a brownie recipe in them, our chocolate brownie has been on the menu since the beginning of the restaurant so we felt it would be rude not to include it for all those die-hard chocolate brownie fans. You can substitute ordinary flour if you don't need to make your brownie gluten free.

Makes one large tray brownie

- 200g dark chocolate (minimum 70% cocoa solids)
- 250g unsalted butter, cut into chunks
- 5 eggs
- 375g caster sugar
- 100g gluten-free flour
- 4 tbsp cocoa powder
- 1½ tsp baking powder
- ½ tsp fine sea salt
- 150g flaked almonds

Preheat the oven to 160°C/gas mark 2–3. Use a baking tray approximately 20cm x 30cm and 2.5cm deep; grease it and line with baking paper.

Place a glass bowl over a pan of simmering water, but make sure the bottom of the bowl is above the level of the water. Break up the chocolate and put it in the bowl with the butter. Allow it to melt, then stir with a wooden spoon and mix it well.

In a large bowl, whisk the eggs and sugar until pale and fluffy. Carefully spoon the chocolate mix into the eggs and sugar, and stir gently to combine. Sift the flour, cocoa powder, baking powder and salt into the egg and chocolate mix and carefully fold them through.

Put the mixture into the baking tray and scatter the almonds on top. Cook the brownie in the oven for 35–40 minutes or until just firm to the touch. When it is cooked, remove it from the oven and allow it to cool for 10 minutes. Then cut it into squares and cool them completely on a wire rack.

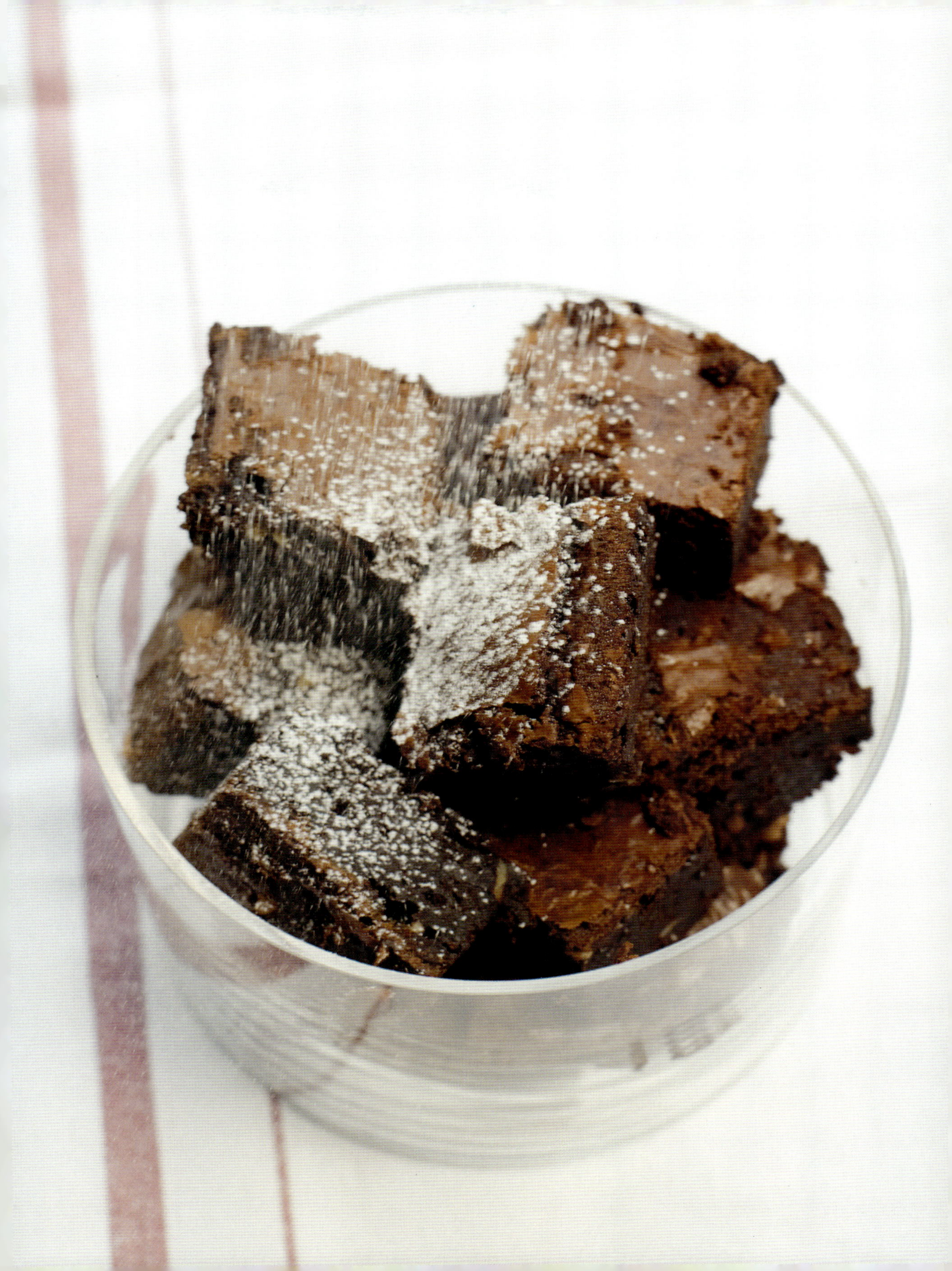

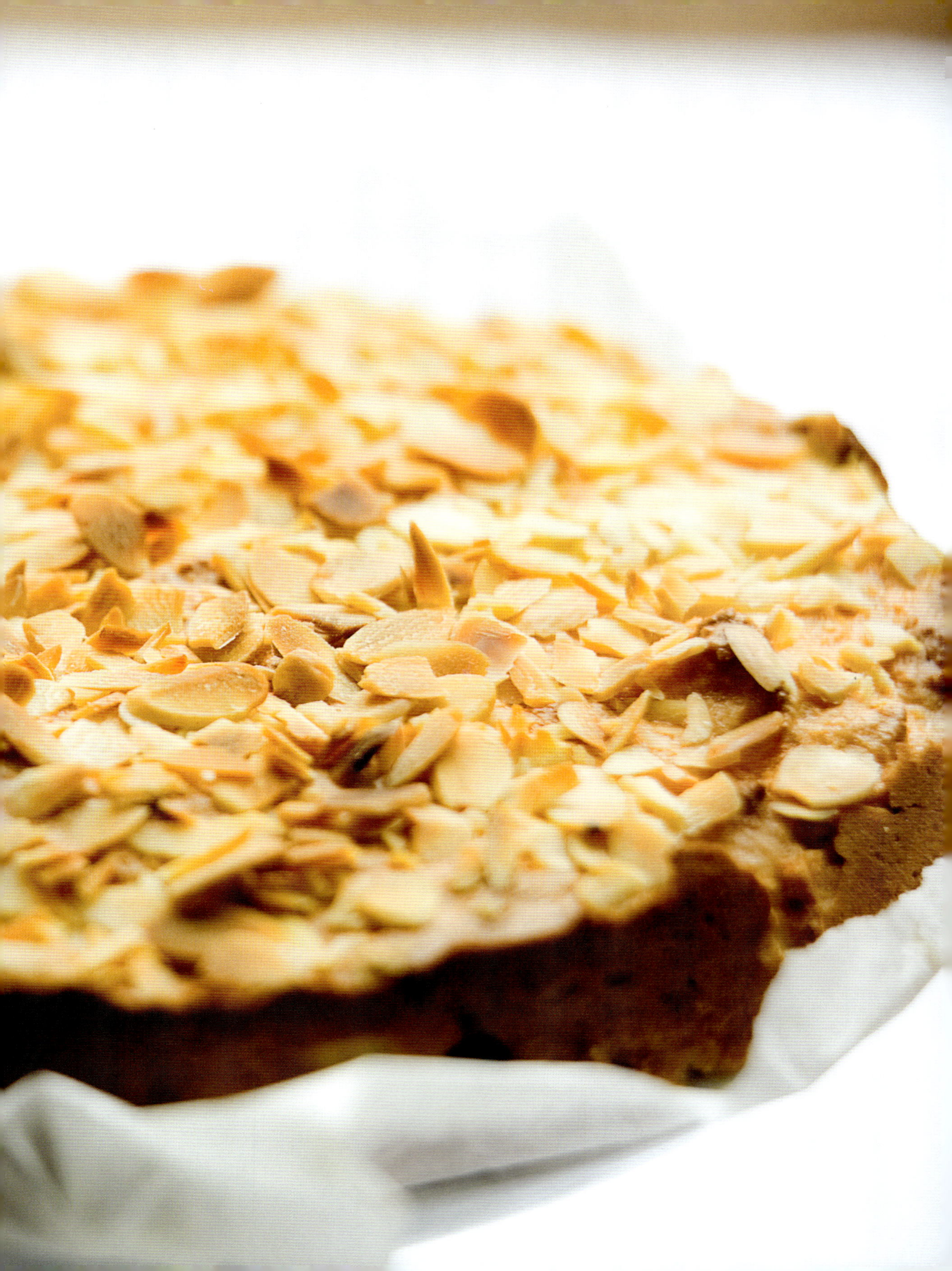

GF, N
Fileto's gluten-free almond cake

Fileto has worked at Food for Friends for nearly as long as Ramin and I have owned it, and it is not unusual to find him in the pastry section experimenting and coming up with new recipes. This is one of his lovely cakes which we sell for afternoon tea.

Makes one 30cm cake

14 egg whites
1 tsp salt
150g sugar
350g ground almonds
zest of 2 oranges
50g flaked almonds

Preheat the oven to 180°C/gas mark 4. Grease and line a 30cm cake tin, spring-bottomed if possible, with baking paper.

Whisk the egg whites with the salt until they stand in soft peaks. While whisking, gradually add the sugar. Keep whisking until the mixture is firm, glossy and thick. Carefully fold in the ground almonds and orange zest with a small metal spoon.

Pour the mixture into the cake tin and sprinkle the flaked almonds on top. Bake the cake in the oven until it is golden on top, which should take approximately 25 minutes; insert a skewer in the middle to check that it is cooked in the middle. Remove it from the oven, and cool it in the tin for 10 minutes before turning it out and allowing it to finish cooling on a wire rack.

Jane's simple baklava-style coconut cake

This is a Middle Eastern recipe which is simple and so popular – even with the kids, who swear they don't like coconut. It can be served warm with ice cream or custard as a dessert, or cool as an afternoon tea cake. It keeps really well in a tightly sealed cake tin or plastic container.

Serves 4–6

115g unsalted butter
175g sugar
50g plain flour
150g semolina
75g desiccated coconut
175ml milk
1 tsp baking powder
1 tsp vanilla essence
toasted almonds to decorate

For the syrup:
1 tbsp lemon juice
115g caster sugar
150ml water

Preheat the oven to 180°C/gas mark 4. Line a baking tray 30 by 20cm and 2cm deep with greased baking paper.

Make the syrup. Put the lemon juice, sugar and water in a saucepan, stir to mix and then bring to a boil. Simmer for 8–10 minutes until the syrup has thickened, then take the pan off the heat. Allow it to cool down and then chill it in the fridge.

Melt the butter in a saucepan. Take it off the heat and add the sugar, flour, semolina, coconut, milk, baking powder and vanilla essence, and mix thoroughly. Pour this into the baking tin immediately and smooth the top. Bake it in the oven for 30–35 minutes until the top is golden brown.

Take the cake out of the oven, and score it into diamond-shaped pieces. Then pour the chilled syrup all over the cake and decorate each piece with an almond. Serve it as a warm dessert, or allow it to cool down in the tin and store the pieces in a air-tight container.

N, GF
Moist pistachio and polenta cake

Makes one 23cm cake

100g fine polenta
200g ground pistachios
1 tsp baking powder
3 eggs
120g caster sugar
100ml sunflower or vegetable oil
100g unsalted butter, melted and cooled
juice and grated zest of 1 lemon
juice and grated zest of 1 orange

Preheat the oven to 180°C/gas mark 4. Grease and line a 23cm loose-bottomed cake tin.

Mix the polenta, pistachios and baking powder together in a bowl. Using a mixer, whisk the eggs and sugar together, then slowly whisk in the oil and butter. Whisk in the pistachio mixture, then add the fruit juices and zest.

Transfer the mixture to the cake tin and bake for 40 minutes. The cake should be slightly underdone in the middle, as it will settle out of the oven. Allow it to cool in the tin for 10 minutes before turning it out and cooling it on a wire rack.

GF
Coffee-spiked white and dark chocolate brownie

Makes one large tray brownie

250g good quality white chocolate
150g gluten-free flour
200g dark chocolate (minimum 70% cocoa solids)
2 tbsp instant coffee dissolved in 1 tbsp hot water
250g unsalted butter, cubed
4 eggs
225g caster sugar
1 tsp vanilla extract

Preheat the oven to 160°C/gas mark 2–3. Take a baking tray approximately 20cm x 30cm and 2.5cm deep, grease it and line with baking paper.

Put a glass bowl over a pan of simmering water, ensuring the base of the bowl and the water do not touch. Break up the white chocolate and melt it in the bowl. Once it has melted, stir in 50g of the gluten-free flour and put it to one side. Place a second bowl over the saucepan of simmering water and melt the dark chocolate with the coffee mixture and butter.

Using a mixer or electric hand whisk, beat the eggs, sugar and vanilla extract until light and creamy. Sieve the rest of the gluten-free flour into the mixture and carefully fold it through. Add the dark chocolate mixture and stir it through, then pour it into the baking tray.

Put blobs of the white chocolate mix randomly over the brownie. Use a skewer or sharp knife to draw lines across the brownie to make the white chocolate bleed into the dark chocolate mix and give it a marbled effect.

Bake in the oven for approximately 30 minutes or until the centre is firm and puffed up a little. When it is cooked, remove it from the oven and allow it to cool for 10 minutes. Then cut it into squares; cool them completely on a wire rack.

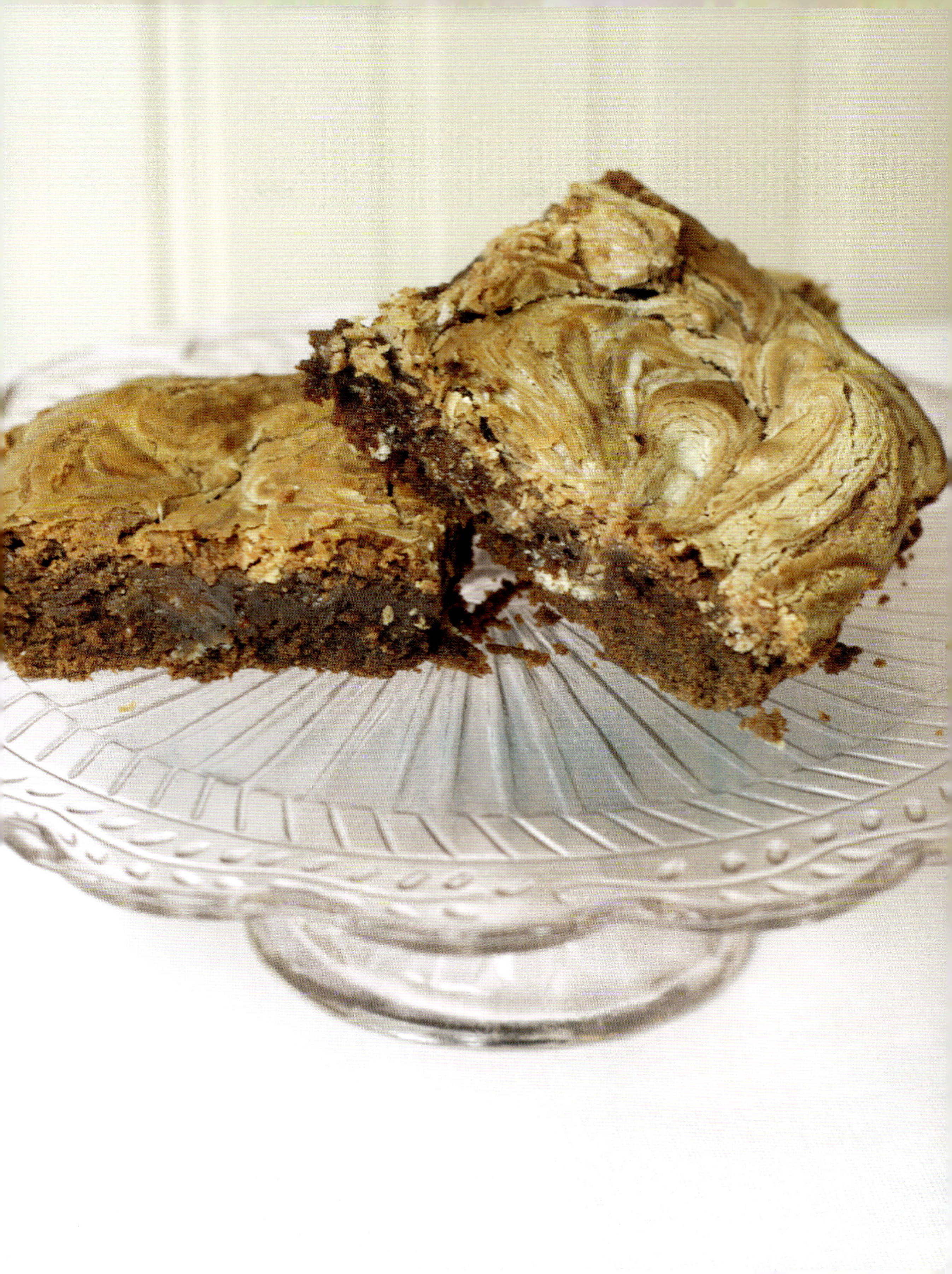

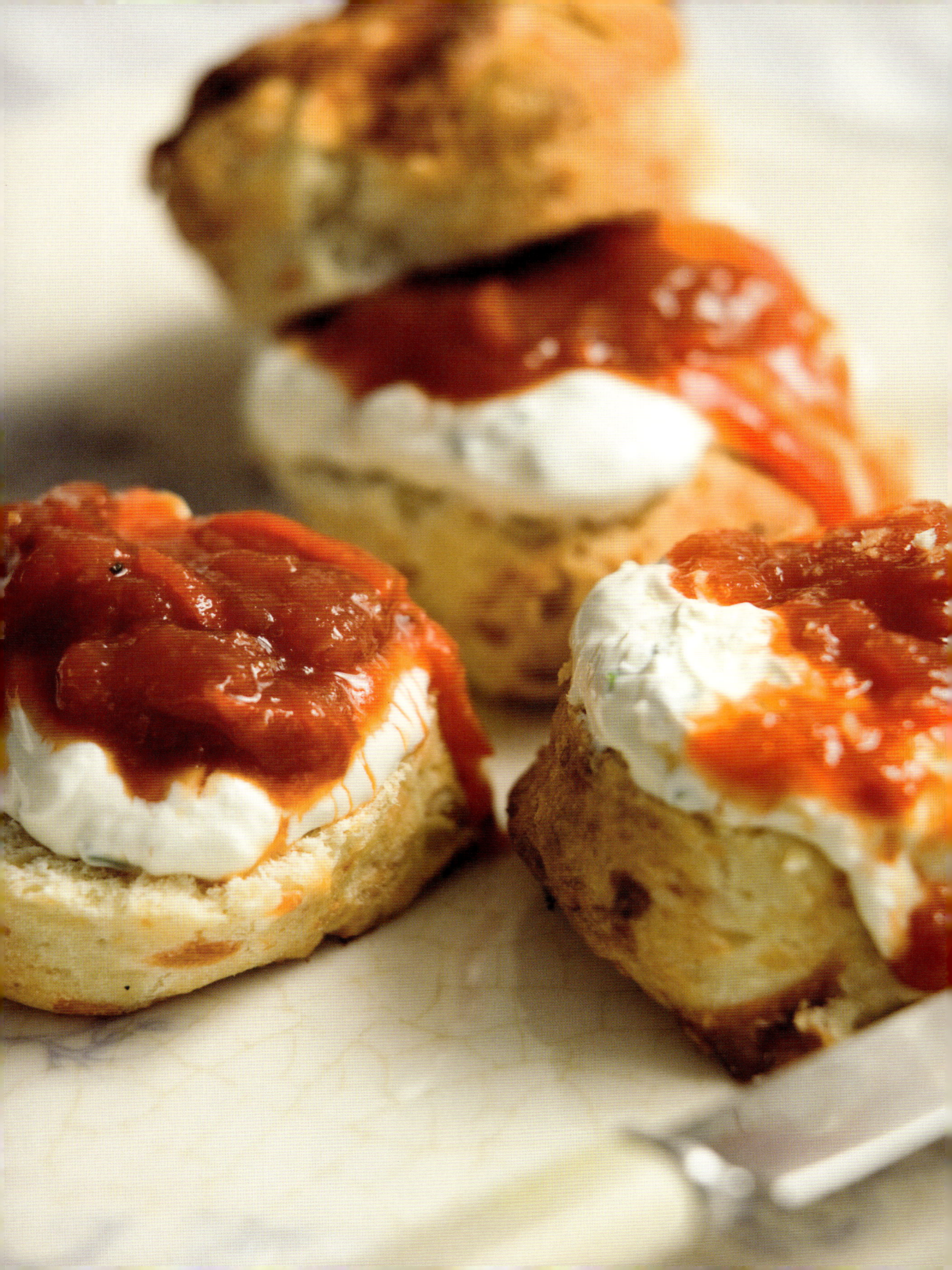

Afternoon tea scones

Every day at three o'clock at Food for Friends the smell of freshly baked scones wafts through the restaurant from the kitchens ready for afternoon tea service. Below are our savoury and sweet scones, with a vegan option.

Cheese scones

Makes 6 large scones

125g unsalted butter, cubed, at room temperature
500g self-raising flour
50g grated cheese, a mixture of cheddar and parmesan-style vegetarian cheese, plus some cheddar for topping
150–175ml warm milk

Preheat the oven to 200°C/gas mark 6.

Using a free-standing mixer, if possible, rub the butter and flour together until they resemble breadcrumbs. Add the grated cheeses and mix them in. With the mixer on, gradually add the warm milk. Check the dough for dryness as you go and add some more milk or flour if necessary; you want to end up with a fairly soft mix but not a sticky one, as it will melt in the oven.

Roll the dough out until it is about 2.5cm thick, and cut out the shapes using an 8cm cutter or pastry ring. Brush the tops with a little milk, sprinkle a little grated cheddar on each one and bake for 15 minutes or until golden in colour.

We like to serve these with sour cream and the chilli jam from page 14.

Sultana scones (VO)

Makes 6 large scones

175g unsalted butter
500g self-raising flour
50g caster sugar
a handful of sultanas, soaked in brandy
150–175ml warm milk

Make these in the same way as the cheese scones, but adding the sultanas and sugar instead of the cheeses.

You can also make vegan scones by replacing the butter with vegan margarine, and the milk with soya milk.

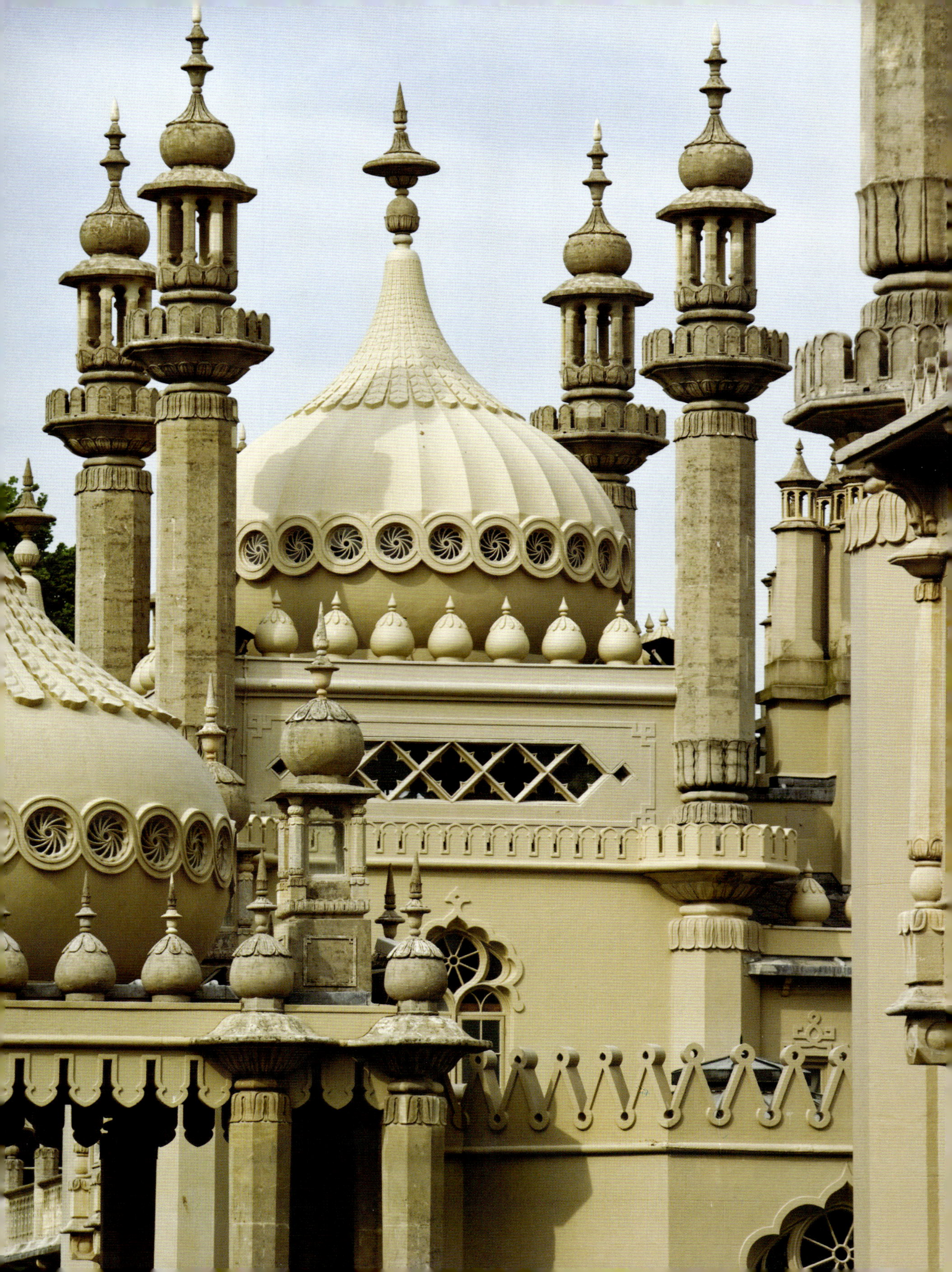

Index

almonds
   almond cake, gluten free, 163
   Persian rice with sour cherries, chickpeas, pistachios and almonds, 73
amae sauce, 68–9
artichokes
   asparagus, dolcelatte, artichoke, petit pois and mint risotto, 75
   ricotta, artichoke, spinach and parmesan bakes, 44
   warm asparagus, artichoke and marinated roasted aubergine salad, 20–21
   whole globe artichoke with dips, 43
asparagus
   asparagus, dolcelatte, artichoke, petit pois and mint risotto, 75
   asparagus and parmesan cream, 43
   butternut risotto fritters with marinated roasted aubergines and chargrilled asparagus spears, 78–9
   chargrilled, 46, 118–19
   puy lentil, aubergine and red wine moussaka, 56–57
   spicy lentil and sun-dried tomato burgers, 84–85
   warm asparagus, artichoke and marinated roasted aubergine salad, 20–21
aubergines
   aubergine croque monsieur, 80–81
   aubergine, pomegranate and walnut bake, 65
   butternut risotto fritters with marinated roasted aubergines and chargrilled asparagus, 78–79
avocados
   papaya and avocado salad, 19
   warm haloumi, wasabi-cashew nut, mango and avocado salad, 18

Baileys ice cream, 147
baked stuffed tomatoes with paella rice, 108
baklava-style coconut cake, 164
balsamic dressing, 8
basic tomato sauce, 4
basil
   basil-infused oil, 43
   basil, parmesan and lemon thyme pesto, 7
   basil, rocket and pine-nut pesto, 7
   basil sauce, 92–93
   pistachio, cashew, rocket and basil pesto, 6
   sun-dried tomato, pitted black olive, basil and pine-nut pesto, 7
   sun-dried tomato and smoked cheese beignet, 92–93
basmati rice, orange-scented, 117
Béarnaise sauce, 46
beetroot
   beetroot and chilli jam, 98–99
   beetroot and mint dip, 40
   beetroot soup with a spinach and feta salsa, 30
   oven-baked beetroot gnocchi with melted cherry vine tomatoes, roasted fennel and pesto, 58–59
black olives
   in lemon and rosemary, 11
   with roasted red pepper and capers, 11
   sun-dried tomato and black olive sausages, 95
   sun-dried tomato, pitted black olive, basil and pine-nut pesto, 7
blue cheese
   butternut squash, sweet potato and dolcelatte lasagne, 64
   porcini and blue cheese crispy arancini, 98–99
   watercress, orange, grapefruit and dolcelatte salad, 27

bread and butter puddings, white chocolate, 143
broccoli bake, 113
brownies, chocolate, 160, 166
brown rice, 125
burgers
   puy lentil, goat's cheese and olive, 82
   spicy lentil and sun-dried tomato, 84–85
butter bean and carrot soup with brazil nuts and thyme, 34
butternut squash
   butternut risotto fritters, 78–79
   butternut squash, sweet potato and dolcelatte lasagne, 64
   butternut tahini dip, 40
   feta, butternut squash, caramelised onion and cashew-nut wellingtons, 132
   spicy potato, butternut squash, pea and paneer curry, 116
   with sun-dried tomato and smoked cheese beignet, 92–93

caramelised shallot and pumpkin tarte tatin, 109
cardamom
   cardamom and white chocolate truffles, 157
   saffron and cardamom crème caramel, 144
carrot and butter bean soup with brazil nuts and thyme, 34
cashew nuts
   cashew and chilli dressing, 19
   feta, butternut squash, caramelised onion and cashew-nut wellingtons, 132
   pistachio, cashew, rocket and basil pesto, 6
   roasted wasabi-cashew nuts, 13
cassava and puy lentil shepherdess pie, 127

cauliflower kuku, 48
chargrilled asparagus, 46
cheese scones, 169
cherries, chickpeas, pistachios and almonds with Persian rice, 73
chervil, chestnut mushroom and pine nut paté, 49
chestnut and sweet potato soup, 37
chestnut mushroom, chervil and pine nut paté, 49
chilled gazpacho, 35
chilli
    beetroot and chilli jam, 98–99
    cashew and chilli dressing, 19
    chilli tomato sauce, 4
    chilli and lime dressing, 26
    jam, 14
    lemon grass and chilli oil, 10
    mixed roasted nuts, sultanas and orange-peel chilli, 13
    pinto bean chilli, 74
    roasted pepper and chilli hummus, 40
    sweet chilli dipping sauce, 87
chocolate
    brownies, 160, 166
    molten pots, 146
    sauce, 138
    torte, pear and tofu, 140
    triple white and dark chocolate semifreddo, 149
    truffles, 157
    white chocolate bread and butter puddings, 143
Christmas pudding, 134
chutney, pear and plum, 14
coconut
    cake, 164
    rice, 124
    spiced pumpkin, coconut and ginger soup, 32
coffee-spiked white and dark chocolate brownie, 166
coriander
    jasmine coriander rice, 118–119
    lemon and coriander dressing, 8
couscous, herby, 121
cranberry crèmes brûlées, 145
crème caramel, saffron and cardamom, 144

crèmes brûlées, cranberry, 145
croque monsieur, aubergine, 80–81
curry
    Malaysian vegetable, 118–119
    spicy potato, butternut squash, pea and paneer, 116
    Thai green, 123–124

dark chocolate
    coffee-spiked white and dark chocolate brownie, 166
    triple white and dark chocolate semifreddo, 149
    truffles, 157
dips, 40, 43
dolcelatte
    asparagus, dolcelatte, artichoke, petit pois and mint risotto, 75
    butternut squash, sweet potato and dolcelatte lasagne, 66
    dolcelatte and truffle oil dressing, 23
    sweet potato, spinach and dolcelatte pie, 112
    watercress, orange, grapefruit and dolcelatte salad, 27
dressings, 8

fennel, cherry vine tomatoes and pesto with oven-baked beetroot gnocchi, 58–59
feta
    beetroot soup with a spinach and feta salsa, 30
    feta, butternut squash, caramelised onion and cashew-nut wellingtons, 132
    stuffed portobello mushrooms, 105
figs
    poached, 149
    rocket and fig garnish, 45
filo parcels, new potato and mushroom supreme, 106–107
flavoured oils, 10

garlic
    pan-fried garlic spinach, 113
    rosemary and garlic oil, 10
    spring onion and roasted garlic mash, 80–81

gazpacho, 35
ginger, spiced pumpkin and coconut soup, 32
globe artichoke with dips, 43
gluten-free almond cake, 163
gnocchi
    oven-baked beetroot gnocchi, 58–59
    spinach and ricotta gnocchi carbonara, 54
goat's cheese
    double-baked soufflés, 113
    puy lentil goat's cheese and olive burgers, 82
    shallow-fried crispy balls of, 45
grapefruit, watercress, orange and dolcelatte salad, 27
gravy, red wine and date, 131
Greek yoghurt, raspberry and honey millefeuille, 153
green beans, spinach and portobello mushrooms with penne, 55
green curry, Thai, 123–124
green olives
    in fresh herbs, lemon and chilli, 11
    in orange zest, mint and cumin, 11

haloumi, wasabi-cashew nut, mango and avocado salad, warm, 18
herby couscous, 121
honey-glazed walnuts, 13
honey, raspberry and Greek yoghurt millefeuille, 153
hot toffee sauce, 150
hummus, roasted pepper and chilli, 40

ice cream
    Baileys, 147
    base recipe, 154

jam
    beetroot and chilli, 98–99
    chilli, 14
jasmine coriander rice, 118–119

kuku, Persian cauliflower, 48

lasagne
    butternut squash, sweet potato and dolcelatte, 64
    roasted Mediterranean vegetable, 61
lemon
    lemon and coriander dressing, 8
    spinach, lentil and lemon soup, 33
lemon grass and chilli oil, 10
lemon thyme, basil and parmesan pesto, 7
lentils
    puy lentil, aubergine and red wine moussaka, 56–57
    red lentil, sweet pepper and mozzarella savoury cakes, 90
    shepherdess pie, 127
    spicy lentil and sun-dried tomato burger, 84–85
    spinach, lentil and lemon soup, 33

Malaysian vegetable curry, 118–119
mango
    dressing, 8
    salad, 87
    warm haloumi, wasabi-cashew nut, mango and avocado salad, 18
marinating olives, 11
marmalade, red onion, 45
mash, spring onion and roasted garlic, 80–81
Mediterranean vegetable lasagne, 61
mince pies, 135
mint, asparagus, dolcelatte, artichoke and petit pois risotto, 75
mirin dressing, 8
mixed roasted nuts, sultanas and orange-peel chilli, 13
moist pistachio and polenta cake, 165
moussaka, puy lentil, aubergine and red wine, 56–57
mozzarella
    portobello mushroom pie with spinach and smoked mozzarella, 110
    red lentil, sweet pepper and mozzarella savoury cakes, 90
mushrooms
    baby carrot and mushroom stroganoff, 125
    chestnut mushroom, chervil and pine nut paté, 49
    duxelles, 88–89
    new potato and mushroom supreme filo parcels, 106–107
    paprika-flavoured mushrooms with smoked tofu and pan-fried polenta, 70
    penne with spinach, portobello mushrooms and green beans, 55
    porcini and blue cheese crispy arancini, 98–99
    portobello mushroom pie, 110
    sautéed wild mushroom, poached pear and walnut salad, 22–23
    stuffed portobello mushroom, 105

new potato and mushroom supreme filo parcels, 106–107
nuts, toasted, 12–13

oils, flavoured, 10, 43
olives
    black olives in lemon and rosemary, 11
    black olives with roasted red pepper and capers, 11
    green olives in fresh herbs, lemon and chilli, 11
    green olives in orange zest, mint and cumin, 11
    marinating, 11
    puy lentil, goat's cheese and olive burgers, 82
    sun-dried tomato and black olive sausages, 95
    sun-dried tomato, pitted black olive, basil and pine-nut pesto, 7
oranges
    mixed roasted nuts, sultanas and orange-peel chilli, 13
    orange-scented basmati rice, 117
    watercress, orange, grapefruit and dolcelatte salad, 27
oven-baked beetroot gnocchi, 58–9

paneer, potato, butternut squash and pea curry, 116
panzanella salad with roast vegetables, 25
papaya and avocado salad with a cashew nut and chilli dressing, 19
pappardelle, 52
paprika-flavoured mushrooms with smoked tofu and pan-fried polenta, 70
parmesan-style vegetarian cheese
    asparagus and parmesan cream, 43
    basil, parmesan and lemon thyme pesto, 7
    crisps, 37
    ricotta, artichoke, spinach and parmesan bakes, 44
    spinach, parmesan and pine nut sausages, 96
paté, chestnut mushroom, chervil and pine nut, 49
pears
    pear and plum chutney, 15
    pear and tofu chocolate torte, 140
    spiced pickled, 14
    sautéed wild mushroom, poached pear and walnut salad, 22
peas
    asparagus, dolcelatte, artichoke, petit pois and mint risotto, 75
    creamed peas and spinach, 88–89
    spicy potato, butternut squash, pea and paneer curry, 116
penne with spinach, portobello mushrooms and green beans, 55
peppers
    red lentil, sweet pepper and mozzarella savoury cakes, 90
    roasted pepper and chilli hummus, 40
Persian cauliflower kuku, 48
Persian rice with sour cherries, chickpeas, pistachios and almonds, 73
pestos, 6–7
pine nuts
    basil, rocket and pine nut pesto, 7
    chestnut mushroom, chervil and pine nut paté, 49
    roasted, 13
    spinach, parmesan and pine nut sausages, 96
    sun-dried tomato, pitted black olive, basil and pine nut pesto, 7

pinto bean chilli, 74
pistachios
    Persian rice with sour cherries, chickpeas, pistachios and almonds, 73
    pistachio and polenta cake, 165
    pistachio, cashew, rocket and basil pesto, 6
    pistachio pesto, 117
pitted black olive, sun-dried tomato, basil and pine-nut pesto, 7
plum and pear chutney, 14
poached egg with a sweet potato and carrot rosti and mushroom duxelles, 88–89
polenta with paprika-flavoured mushrooms and smoked tofu, 70
pomegranate, aubergine and walnut bake, 65
pomelo and star fruit salad, Thai, 26
porcini and blue cheese crispy arancini, 98–99
portobello mushrooms
    penne with spinach, portobello mushrooms and green beans, 55
    pie, 110
    stuffed, 105
potatoes
    new potato and mushroom supreme filo parcels, 106–107
    potato gratin dauphinois, 131
    wedges, 85
profiteroles, tiramisu, 138
pumpkins
    pumpkin and caramelised shallot tarte tatin, 109
    pumpkin galette, 98
    spiced pumpkin, coconut and ginger soup, 32

raspberry, honey and Greek yoghurt millefeuille, 153
red lentil, sweet pepper and mozzarella savoury cakes, 90
red onion marmalade, 45
red pepper sauce, 3, 62–63
red wine
    puy lentil, aubergine and red wine moussaka, 56–7

    red wine and date gravy, 131
rice
    baby carrot and mushroom stroganoff with brown basmati and wild rice, 125
    coconut rice, 124
    jasmine coriander rice, 118–119
    orange-scented basmati rice, 117
    Persian, 73
ricotta, artichoke, spinach and parmesan bakes, 44
risotto
    of asparagus, dolcelatte, artichoke, petit pois and mint, 75
    butternut risotto fritters, 78–79
roasted pepper and chilli hummus, 40
roasted seeds and nuts, 12–13
roasted tomato sauce, 4
roasted vegetables
    lasagne, 61
    with panzanella salad, 25
rocket
    basil, rocket and pine-nut pesto, 7
    pistachio, cashew, rocket and basil pesto, 6
    rocket and fig garnish, 45
rosemary and garlic oil, 10
rosewater coulis, 141

saffron and cardamom crème caramel, 144
salads, 17–27
salsa, tomato, 43
sausages, 95–96
scones, 169
seeds, toasted, 12–13
shallot and pumpkin tarte tatin, 109
shallow-fried crispy balls of goat's cheese, 45
shepherdess pie, cassava and puy lentil, 127
smoked cheese
    portobello mushroom pie with spinach and smoked mozzarella, 110
    sun-dried tomato and smoked cheese beignet, 92–93
snorkers, 95–96

soufflés, double-baked goat's cheese, 113
soups, 29–37
spiced pickled pears, 15
spiced pumpkin, coconut and ginger soup, 32
spicy dressing, 26
spicy lentil and sun-dried tomato burger, 84–85
spicy potato, butternut squash, pea and paneer curry, 116
spicy teriyaki sauce, 68–69
spinach
    beetroot soup with a spinach and feta salsa, 30
    creamed peas and spinach, 88–89
    pan-fried garlic spinach, 113
    penne with spinach, portobello mushrooms and green beans, 55
    ricotta, artichoke, spinach and parmesan bakes, 44
    spinach and ricotta gnocchi carbonara, 54
    spinach, lentil and lemon soup, 33
    spinach, parmesan and pine nut sausages, 96
    spinach and smoked mozzarella with portobello mushroom pie, 110
    sweet potato, spinach and dolcelatte pie, 112
spring onion and roasted garlic mash, 80–81
squash
    butternut risotto fritters, 78–79
    butternut squash, sweet potato and dolcelatte lasagne, 64
    butternut tahini dip, 40
    feta, butternut squash, caramelised onion and cashew-nut wellingtons, 132
    spicy potato, butternut squash, pea and paneer curry, 116
    with sun-dried tomato and smoked cheese beignet, 92–93
sticky toffee puddings, 150
stir-fried vegetables, 68–69
stock, 2
stroganoff, baby carrot and mushroom, 125

stuffed portobello mushrooms, 105
sultanas
    mixed roasted nuts, sultanas and orange-peel chilli, 13
    sultana scones, 169
Sunday roast, escalopes, 130
sun-dried tomatoes
    spicy lentil and sun-dried tomato burger, 84–85
    sun-dried tomato and black olive sausages, 95
    sun-dried tomato, pitted black olive, basil and pine-nut pesto, 7
    sun-dried tomato and smoked cheese beignet, 92–93
sweet chilli dipping sauce, 87
sweetcorn fritters, 87
sweet peppers
    red lentil, sweet pepper and mozzarella savoury cakes, 90
    roasted pepper and chilli hummus, 40
sweet potatoes
    butternut squash, sweet potato and dolcelatte lasagne, 64
    sweet potato, garlic and rosemary gratin, 62–63
    sweet potato and carrot rosti, 88
    sweet potato and chestnut soup, 37
    sweet potato, spinach and dolcelatte pie, 112
sweet tofu pockets, 102

tagine, vegetable, 120–121
tamarind-coated mixed seeds, 13
teriyaki sauce, 68–69
Thai green curry, 123–124
Thai pomelo and star fruit salad, 26
Thai sweetcorn fritters, 87
tiramisu profiteroles, 138
toasted seeds and nuts, 12–13
toffee puddings, 150
toffee sauce, 150
tofu pockets, 102
tomatoes
    baked stuffed tomatoes with paella rice, 108
    oven-baked beetroot gnocchi with melted cherry vine tomatoes, roasted fennel and pesto, 58–59
    salsa, 43
    sauces, 4, 106–7
    sun-dried tomato and black olive sausages, 95
    sun-dried tomato, pitted black olive, basil and pine-nut pesto, 7
    sun-dried tomato and smoked cheese beignet, 92–93
    tomato salsa, 43
tom ka soup, 31
triple white and dark chocolate semifreddo, 149
truffles, 157
Turkish Delight parfait, 141

vegetable stock, 2
vegetable tagine, 120–121
walnuts
    aubergine, pomegranate and walnut bake, 65
    honey-glazed, 13, 20, 22
warm asparagus, artichoke and marinated roasted aubergine salad with honey walnuts and a tahini dressing, 20–21
warm haloumi, wasabi-cashew nut, mango and avocado salad, 18
wasabi-cashew nuts, roasted, 13
watercress, orange, grapefruit and dolcelatte salad, 27
white chocolate
    bread and butter puddings, 143
    cardamom and white chocolate truffles, 157
    coffee-spiked white and dark chocolate brownie, 166
    white and dark chocolate semifreddo, 149
whole globe artichoke with dips, 43
wild mushrooms
    sautéed wild mushroom, poached pear and walnut salad, 22
wild rice, 125

yoghurt, raspberry and honey millefeuille, 153